DATE DUE

DEMCO 38-296

Standards-Based

SCIENCE

Graphic Organizers, Rubrics, and Writing Prompts for Middle Grade Students

By Imogene Forte
and Sandra Schurr

Incentive Publications, Inc.
Nashville, Tennessee

Graphics by Joe Shibley
Cover by Marta Drayton
Edited by Jean K. Signor

ISBN 0-86530-495-5

PRINTED IN THE UNITED STATES OF AMERICA
www.incentivepublications.com

Table of Contents

PREFACE

Recent research studies have confirmed a belief that intuitive teachers have long held germane to classroom success: when students are meaningfully involved in active learning tasks and in the planning and evaluation of their work, they are more enthusiastic about instructional activities, they learn and retain more, and their overall rate of achievement is greater. With the emphasis placed on measurable achievement as an overriding goal driving school system mandates, curriculum, classroom organization and management, and even instructional practices and procedures, teachers are faced with great challenges. While striving to fulfill societal demands, at the same time they must be creating and using new instructional strategies, procedures, and teaching methods to meet the diverse needs of students with widely varying interests and abilities. With the complexity of daily life in the rapidly changing world in which we live, the global economy, and the growing avalanche of information, middle grades science teachers are turning to student-centered instruction, active learning strategies, and authentic instruction to capture and hold students' interests and attention, and consequently to result in increased achievement levels.

Graphic Organizers

As the body of material to be covered in a given time frame grows more massive and multifaceted, and content demands on students and teachers multiply, graphic organizers are becoming an important component of middle grades science programs.

In the information-saturated classroom of today, sorting and making meaningful use of specific facts, and concepts is becoming an increasingly important skill. Knowing where to go to find information and how to organize it once it is located is the key to processing and making meaningful use of the information gathered. Graphic organizers can be used to: provide visual organization; develop scope and sequence; furnish a plan of action or to aid in assessment; clarify points of interest; and document a process or a series of events.

Their construction and use encourages visual discrimination and organization, use of critical thinking skills, and meta-cognitive reflection. They can be particularly useful in helping middle grade students grasp concepts and skills related to the eight standards established by the National Academy of Sciences.

In other instances, a graphic organizer may be developed as a reporting or review exercise or sometimes as a means of self-assessment when properly used after knowledge has been acquired. Graphic organizers become a valuable and effective instructional and assessment tool. The degree of their effectiveness for both students and teachers is determined by visual clarification of purpose, careful planning, visual organization, and attention to detail.

Rubrics

Authentic assessment, as opposed to more traditional forms of assessment, gives both student and teacher a more realistic picture of gains made, facts, and information processed for retention. Emphasis is placed more on the processing of concepts and information than on the recall of facts. Collecting evidence from authentic assessment exercises, taking place in realistic settings over a period of time, provides students and teachers with the most effective documentation of both skills and content mastery. Traditional measurements of student achievement such as written tests and quizzes, objective end-of-chapter tests, and standardized tests play a major role in the assessment picture as well.

The use of standards-based rubrics in middle grade science classes has proven to be an extremely useful means of authentic assessment for helping students maintain interest and evaluate their own progress.

Rubrics are checklists that contain sets of criteria for measuring the elements of a product, performance, or portfolio. They can be designed as a qualitative measure (holistic rubric) to gauge overall performance of a prompt, or they can be designed as a quantitative measure (analytic rubric) to award points for each of several elements in response to a prompt.

Additional benefits from rubrics are that they: require collaboration among students and teachers; are flexible and allow for individual creativity; make room for individual strengths and weaknesses; minimize competition; are meaningful to parents; allow for flexible time frames; provide multifaceted scoring systems with a variety of formats; can be sources for lively peer discussions and interaction; can include meta-cognitive reflection provisions which encourage self-awareness and critical thinking; and can help teachers determine final grades that are understood by and hold meaning for students.

Writing Prompts

Over the past several years, the significance of journals and writing prompts is well-documented by student and teacher observations. When students write about experiences, knowledge, hopes, fears, memories, and dreams, they broaden and clarify skills and concepts while acquiring new insights into themselves and the big world of which they are a part.

While random journal entries hold their own place of importance in the science classroom, writing prompts designed to elicit specific responses play a vital role in the instructional program.

Journal entries may be presented in many different formats, and may be shared and assessed in a variety of ways. The flexibility of their use and the possibility they provide for integrating instruction cause them to be viewed as an important component of the personalized science program. They may take the form of a file card project, a multimedia presentation, a special notebook, or a diary. They may be private to be discussed with the teacher only, shared with a small group of peers, or the total class. Word prompts can be used in parent-student-teacher conferences, or as take home projects to be shared with parents, saved, or used as a portfolio entry to give an account of a unit of study, field trip, or independent project.

Writing prompts provide the opportunity for students to: create a dialogue with teachers in a meaningful sense; write about self-selected topics of high interest; process and internalize material being learned; communicate with peers; express private opinions, thoughts, and insights without judgment or censorship; write personal reactions or responses to textbook, research assignments, group discussion, and experiences; make record of what and how they are learning and what it means to them; develop a source book of ideas and thoughts related to a specific topic; question material being studied and record answers as they are uncovered; assess their academic or social progress; and engage in meta-cognitive reflection on new skills and concepts being acquired and record plans for further exploration.

These standards-based graphic organizers, writing prompts, and rubrics have been designed to provide busy teachers with a bank of resources from which to draw as the need arises. The eight standards developed by the National Academy of Sciences have been incorporated throughout all activities. For ease in planning, the matrix on pages 122–123 provides a complete correlation of activities to these standards.

Graphic Organizers

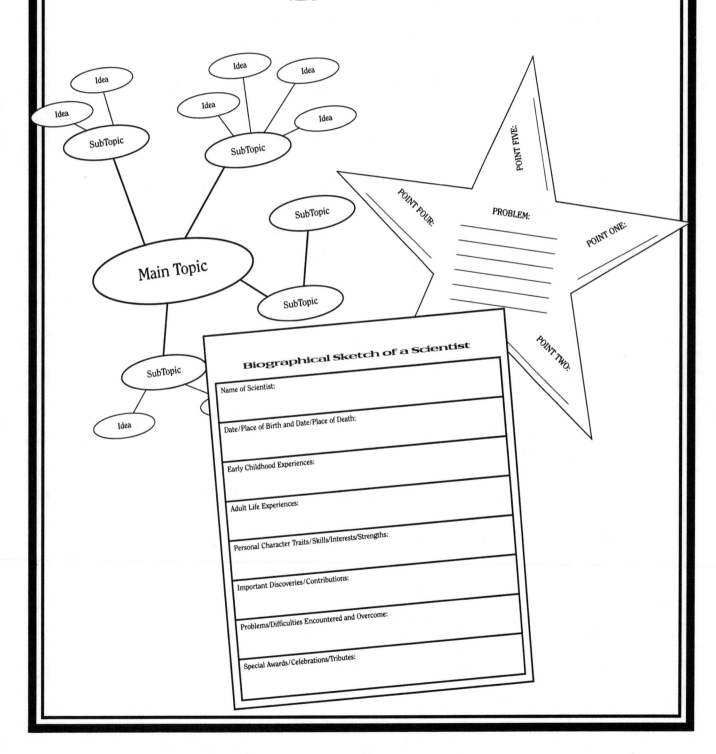

Biographical Sketch of a Scientist

Name of Scientist:

Date/Place of Birth and Date/Place of Death:

Early Childhood Experiences:

Adult Life Experiences:

Personal Character Traits/Skills/Interests/Strengths:

Important Discoveries/Contributions:

Problems/Difficulties Encountered and Overcome:

Special Awards/Celebrations/Tributes:

GUIDELINES
FOR USING GRAPHIC ORGANIZERS

1. Graphic organizers have many purposes; they can be used for curriculum planning, helping students process information, and pre- or post-assessment tasks. Determine which types of graphic organizers are best for each purpose.

2. Graphic organizers are a performance-based model of assessment and make excellent artifacts for inclusion in a portfolio. Decide which concepts in your discipline are best represented by the use of these organizers.

3. Use graphic organizers to help students focus on important concepts while omitting extraneous details.

4. Use graphic organizers as visual pictures to help the student remember key ideas.

5. Use graphic organizers to connect visual language with verbal language in active learning settings.

6. Use graphic organizers to enhance recall of important information.

7. Use graphic organizers to provide student motivation and relieve student boredom.

8. Use graphic organizers to show and explain relationships between and among varied content areas.

9. Use graphic organizers to make traditional lesson plans more interactive and more appealing to the visual learner.

10. Use graphic organizers to break down complex ideas through concise and structured visuals.

11. Use graphic organizers to help students note patterns and clarify ideas.

12. Use graphic organizers to help students better understand the concept of part to whole.

13. Emphasize the use of graphic organizers to stimulate creative thinking.

14. Make sure there is a match between the type of organizer and the content being taught.

15. Make sure that using a graphic organizer is the best use of time when teaching a concept.

16. Use a wide variety of graphic organizers and use them collaboratively whenever possible.

Standards-Based SCIENCE Graphic Organizers, Rubrics, and Writing Prompts for Middle Grade Students

The ABC's of Science

DIRECTIONS: Science covers so many topics from A to Z that it is sometimes helpful to organize these topics according to the three major divisions in science referred to as Life Science, Physical Science, and Earth/Space Science. Complete one of the ABC Sheets for each of the three major science areas by listing a topic (or topics) in each category for all 26 letters of the alphabet.

See page 25 for reproducible copy.

The ABC's of Science

A _____
B _____
C _____
D _____
E _____
F _____
G _____
H _____
I _____
J _____
K _____
L _____
M _____
N _____
O _____
P _____
Q _____
R _____
S _____
T _____
U _____
V _____
W _____
X _____
Y _____
Z _____

Attribute Grid

DIRECTIONS : Use this grid to either analyze or compare and contrast different attributes, criteria, characteristics, or qualities of varied objects, events, places, or things. Write in the attributes, criteria, characteristics, or qualities across the top of the grid and the objects, events, places, or things down the side of the grid.

See page 26 for reproducible copy.

Science Topic: _____

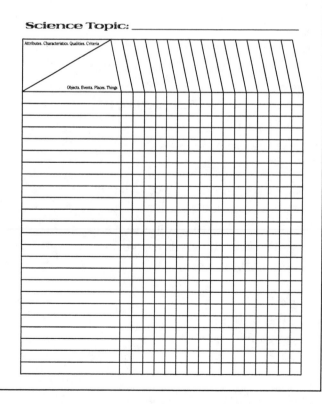

Attributes. Characteristics. Qualities. Criteria

Objects. Events. Places. Things

Standards-Based SCIENCE Graphic Organizers, Rubrics, and Writing Prompts for Middle Grade Students

Biographical Sketch of a Scientist

DIRECTIONS: Outline the life of an important scientist, inventor, or researcher undergoing study by using this chart to record and profile the key ideas gleaned from one's readings or research. This information can then be rewritten into a formal biographical sketch or report.

See page 27 for reproducible copy.

Biographical Sketch of a Scientist

Name of Scientist:
Date/Place of Birth and Date/Place of Death:
Early Childhood Experiences:
Adult Life Experiences:
Personal Character Traits/Skills/Interests/Strengths:
Important Discoveries/Contributions:
Problems/Difficulties Encountered and Overcome:
Special Awards/Celebrations/Tributes:

Cause/Effect Fishbone Map

DIRECTIONS: Science is the discipline of cause and effect from many points of view. It seems that for every action there is an equal and opposite reaction.
(What famous scientist said that?)

Use this fishbone map to record a series of science-oriented cause and effect situations that eventually lead to a result or set of results. Record details where appropriate to do so.

See page 28 for reproducible copy.

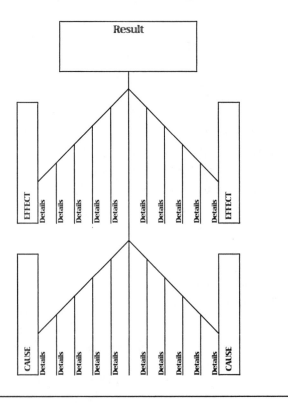

Charting Science Skills

DIRECTIONS: As you complete a hands-on science activity, use this graphic organizer to chart what you did and how you did it. This may be used for experiments, observations, lab activities, investigations, or field studies.

See page 29 for reproducible copy.

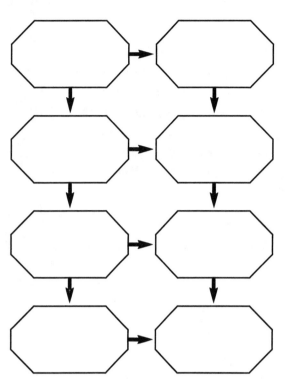

A Concept Builder

DIRECTIONS: Complete this diagram to explore a science-related concept or big idea. List the major concept in the top circle, supporting ideas in the squares below the circle, and the important details or examples in the rectangle at the bottom.

See page 30 for reproducible copy.

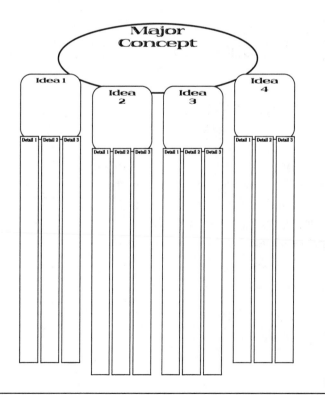

Standards-Based SCIENCE Graphic Organizers, Rubrics, and Writing Prompts for Middle Grade Students

The Cycle Graph

DIRECTIONS: Cycles are very important in the study of science. Use this circle organizer to record the various steps in a cycle of your choice. Feel free to insert additional items in the cycle if it requires more than six steps to complete.

See page 31 for reproducible copy.

Topic or Title

6.

1.

5.

2.

4.

3.

Discussion Guide

DIRECTIONS: Before participating in an active discussion group where you are to trade information and hear what others have to say about the overall science topic assigned or agreed upon, prepare some answers to each of the questions suggested by the graphic organizer in order to provide the group with both a consistent agenda to follow and some ideas to share.

See page 32 for reproducible copy.

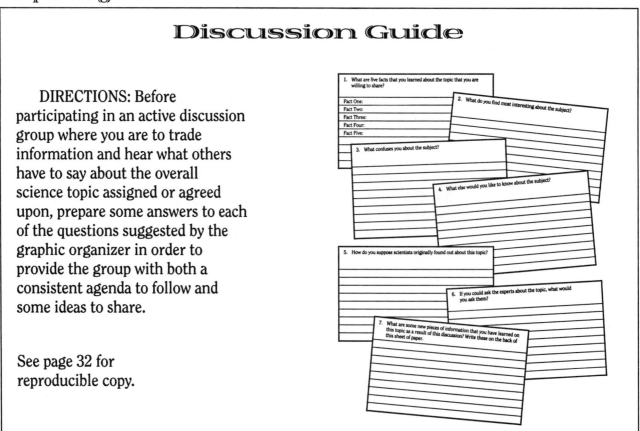

1. What are five facts that you learned about the topic that you are willing to share?

Fact One:
Fact Two:
Fact Three:
Fact Four:
Fact Five:

2. What do you find most interesting about the subject?

3. What confuses you about the subject?

4. What else would you like to know about the subject?

5. How do you suppose scientists originally found out about this topic?

6. If you could ask the experts about the topic, what would you ask them?

7. What are some new pieces of information that you have learned on this topic as a result of this discussion? Write these on the back of this sheet of paper.

Event/Outcome Graph

DIRECTIONS: Use this graph to record a series of scientific events that led to a given set of outcomes or results. Record the event on the horizontal axis and the related outcome/result on the vertical axis.

See page 33 for reproducible copy.

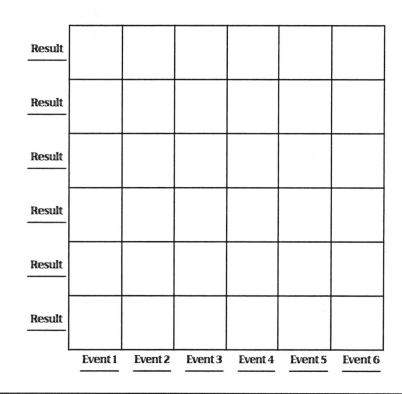

Result

Result

Result

Result

Result

Result

Event 1   Event 2   Event 3   Event 4   Event 5   Event 6

Fact, Comment, and Question Textbook Survey

DIRECTIONS: Use this template to survey and write down the important facts from a textbook selection you are reading. For each paragraph, record the main fact given, a personal comment/reactions/opinion about the stated fact, and a question to ask yourself that will help you remember each fact.

See page 34 for reproducible copy.

Fact
Comment/Reaction/Opinion
Question

Fact
Comment/Reaction/Opinion
Question

Fact
Comment/Reaction/Opinion
Question

Standards-Based SCIENCE Graphic Organizers, Rubrics, and Writing Prompts for Middle Grade Students

The 5 W's and How of Scientific Theories, Principles, and Laws

DIRECTIONS: Use this diagram to help you remember the five W's (Who, What, When, Where, Why) and How of an important scientific theory, principle, or law. This graphic organizer is similar to the inverted pyramid often used in analyzing a newspaper article.

See page 35 for reproducible copy.

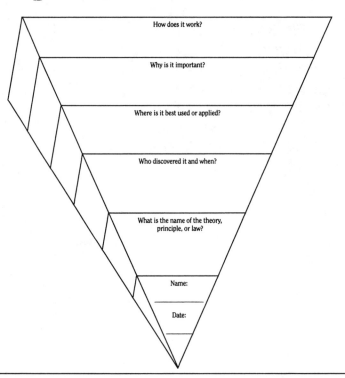

Flowcharting

DIRECTIONS: Use the flowcharting symbols shown to construct a sequencing of events to explain a scientific process or phenomenon. Note how the different shapes, lines, and arrows are drawn to indicate different symbols and words.

See page 36 for reproducible copy.

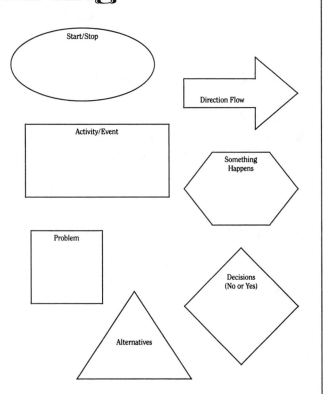

Standards-Based SCIENCE Graphic Organizers, Rubrics, and Writing Prompts for Middle Grade Students

Hypothesis-Proof-Opinion Chart

Use this chart to record your notes when forming an hypothesis about a scientific idea, discovery, or experiment. State the hypothesis, give statements of proof to either support or negate the hypothesis, and then summarize your opinion-proof notes in a concluding paragraph.

See page 37 for reproducible copy.

Hypothesis/Proof/Opinion Chart	
Hypothesis:	Proof Statements:
Opinion/Proof Notes and Conclusion	

Idea Organizer

DIRECTIONS: Many controversial topics are presented in a science course for discussion and debate. Use this Idea Organizer to write down key ideas, reasons, and conclusions that are generated during a small or large group dialogue.

See page 38 for reproducible copy.

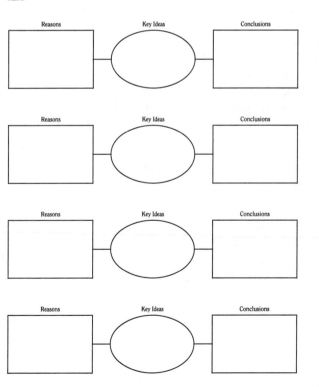

Standards-Based SCIENCE Graphic Organizers, Rubrics, and Writing Prompts for Middle Grade Students

Investigating Significant Event Step by Step

DIRECTIONS: Identify and define the major steps leading up to any significant scientific event, discovery, experiment, or disaster by using this simulated staircase as a graphic organizer. Write a summary statement/conclusion/commentary in the box at the bottom of the page.

See page 39 for reproducible copy.

Statement/Conclusion/Commentary

Log of Scientific Terms

DIRECTIONS: Record all of the important scientific words or terms from a unit of study by writing the word itself in the first box, defining the word in the second box, and illustrating the word (or using the word in a sentence) in the third box.

See page 40 for reproducible copy.

Scientific Term	Definition of Term	Illustration/Sentence of Term
Scientific Term	Definition of Term	Illustration/Sentence of Term
Scientific Term	Definition of Term	Illustration/Sentence of Term
Scientific Term	Definition of Term	Illustration/Sentence of Term
Scientific Term	Definition of Term	Illustration/Sentence of Term
Scientific Term	Definition of Term	Illustration/Sentence of Term

Standards-Based SCIENCE Graphic Organizers, Rubrics, and Writing Prompts for Middle Grade Students

Panel Planner

DIRECTIONS: Plan a panel presentation on a topic studied in science. Choose three people to serve on the panel with you and a moderator whose job it is to both organize the panel's delivery of information and to keep the panel's questions/answers/comments moving along in a smooth and orderly fashion. Write down the topic for the panel presentation, the names and science concepts to be covered by each panel member, and some basic questions the panel moderator can use as needed to facilitate the discussion.

See page 41 for reproducible copy.

Topic for Panel _____

Name of Panel Moderator _____

Question 1: _____
Question 2: _____
Question 3: _____
Question 4: _____

Panel Member One
_____
_____

Panel Member Two
_____
_____

Panel Member Three
_____
_____

Panel Member Four
_____
_____

Picture/Graph Response Sheet

DIRECTIONS: Use this graphic organizer to record individual thoughts about any meaningful picture, photograph, illustration, drawing, diagram, chart, or graph that is encountered in a science textbook or reference book.
It has been said many times that "a picture (or visual) is worth a thousand words."

See page 42 for reproducible copy.

Describe what you see.

Explain what is happening.

Tell why this is happening.

Give reasons why it was chosen for this book.

*Standards-Based SCIENCE Graphic Organizers, Rubrics,
and Writing Prompts for Middle Grade Students*

Position Paper Planner

DIRECTIONS: Use this outline to plan the major ideas and supporting details for a short, but interesting position paper on a science topic that has been assigned or selected by choice. Keep in mind that a position paper is written to convince others how the author feels or reacts to a given situation.

See page 43 for reproducible copy.

Introductory Paragraph

   1. Eye-catching example, startling statement, personal anecdote, dramatic quotation, unusual data/fact to catch reader's attention.

   2. Thesis Statement

Body Paragraph One

   1. Topic Sentence

      2. Supporting Sentence

      3. Supporting Sentence

      4. Supporting Sentence

Body Paragraph Two

   1. Topic Sentence

      2. Supporting Sentence

      3. Supporting Sentence

      4. Supporting Sentence

Body Paragraph Three

   1. Topic Sentence

      2. Supporting Sentence

      3. Supporting Sentence

      4. Supporting Sentence

Concluding Paragraph

   1. Concluding sentence based on thesis statement.

   2. Final statement in form of rhetorical question, point to ponder, or basis for further study.

Problem-Solving Tree

Use this tree to visually depict possible outcomes for any science-related problem under study by charting various advantages and disadvantages to several different but potential solutions. Write a summary conclusion in the squares provided for this purpose at the bottom of each solution figure.

See page 44 for reproducible copy.

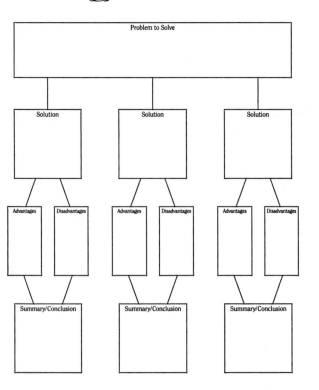

Report Outline
Using Bloom's Taxonomy

DIRECTIONS: Choose a topic for an interesting science report or project and complete each of the tasks listed on the graphic organizer using Bloom's Taxonomy of Cognitive Development as your organizing structure. Keep in mind that these tasks are arranged in a scope and sequence so that each level progresses from lower order thinking skills to higher order thinking skills. Use this graphic organizer as a rough outline for recording key ideas that are included in a more comprehensive product.

See page 45 for reproducible copy.

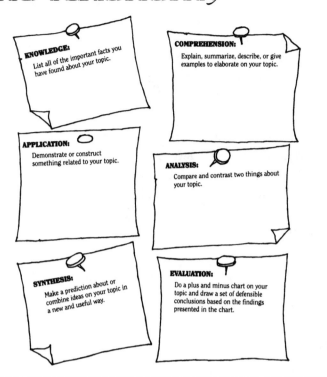

KNOWLEDGE: List all of the important facts you have found about your topic.

COMPREHENSION: Explain, summarize, describe, or give examples to elaborate on your topic.

APPLICATION: Demonstrate or construct something related to your topic.

ANALYSIS: Compare and contrast two things about your topic.

SYNTHESIS: Make a prediction about or combine ideas on your topic in a new and useful way.

EVALUATION: Do a plus and minus chart on your topic and draw a set of defensible conclusions based on the findings presented in the chart.

The Research Regulator

DIRECTIONS: It is important to establish a plan for guiding or regulating one's research on a science topic in order to make the data gathering process more manageable and readable. Use this research tool to plan a project or product.

See page 46 for reproducible copy.

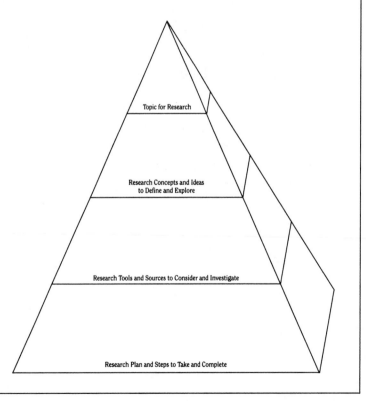

Topic for Research

Research Concepts and Ideas to Define and Explore

Research Tools and Sources to Consider and Investigate

Research Plan and Steps to Take and Complete

Standards-Based SCIENCE Graphic Organizers, Rubrics, and Writing Prompts for Middle Grade Students

Scientific Categories and Their Relationships

DIRECTIONS: Choose a scientific topic for study and list its subcategories and relationships in such a way that one is able to see a scope and sequence to their organizational structure. This graphic organizer should enable the reader to visually see relationships among all circles and lines.

See page 47 for reproducible copy.

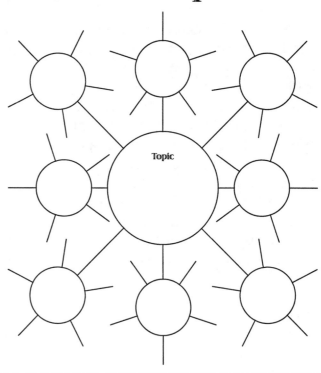

Storyboard

DIRECTIONS: Use this storyboard format to plan a simple oral presentation, chalk talk, or visual display. Decide on a scientific concept or process to explain or demonstrate. Then plan the presentation by drawing a series of illustrations in each box and writing appropriate script for the box, making certain that these pictures and words occur in a specific and logical sequence.

See page 48 for reproducible copy.

1.	6.
2.	7.
3.	8.
4.	9.
5.	10.

Time Line Template

DIRECTIONS: Decide on the important dates to record when investigating a scientific discovery, invention, event, or when researching the life of an important scientist from history. Then write down the specific events that go with each date. This time line pattern can be extended as needed. Note, too, that the vertical lines at the bottom of the graphic organizer can be used for additional notes or comments.

See page 49 for reproducible copy.

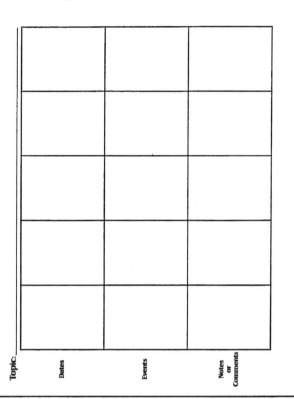

Topic: | Dates | Events | Notes or Comments

The Tools of Science

DIRECTIONS: How many different activities could you do with each of these common tools used by the scientist in his/her daily work? Record as many different functions as you can think of for each item. For example, when a scientist uses a microscope, he/she magnifies, scrutinizes, views, examines, etc.

See page 50 for reproducible copy.

1. Microscope _____
2. Telescope _____
3. Thermometer _____
4. Meter Stick _____
5. Electric Circuit _____
6. Magnet _____
7. Pulley _____
8. Periodic Table _____
9. Beaufort Scale _____
10. Mohs Scale _____
11. Weather Vane _____
12. Bunsen Burner _____
13. Balance Scale _____
14. Prism _____
15. Beaker or Flask _____
16. Magnifying Glass _____
17. Inclined Plane _____
18. Litmus Paper _____
19. Tuning Fork _____

*Standards-Based SCIENCE Graphic Organizers, Rubrics,
and Writing Prompts for Middle Grade Students*

Using Multiple Intelligences to Gather Data for Science Project or Presentation

DIRECTIONS: To gather data and input for a science-related project or presentation, try using the eight different multiple intelligences as an organizing structure or format when locating information on a topic of choice that is both relevant and varied from multiple points of view. Use the questions listed on the graphic organizer as a guideline to get you started.

See pages 51 and 52 for reproducible copy.

1. Verbal/Linguistic Intelligence:
   What books, magazines, newspapers, and other print materials are available for you to review?
   _____

2. Logical/Mathematical Intelligence:
   How can charts, graphs, diagrams, and technology tools help you gather information?
   _____

3. Visual/Spatial Intelligence:
   What pictures, photographs, maps, videos, posters, and other forms of visuals have information about the topic?
   _____

4. Musical/Rhythmic Intelligence:
   How might songs, raps, and audio tapes relate to your topic?
   _____

5. Bodily-Kinesthetic Intelligence:
   What computer software, Internet web sites, skits, dances, or physical/sporting events could serve you as reliable resources?
   _____

6. Interpersonal Intelligence:
   What family members, friends, teachers, experts, or community groups/organizations/institutions are there for you to interview in person, by telephone, or through chat rooms?
   _____

7. Intrapersonal Intelligence:
   What personal experiences, readings, feelings, opinions, or ideas do you have on the topic that you can pull from?
   _____

8. Naturalist Intelligence:
   How do Mother Nature and wildlife relate to your topic?
   _____

Venn Diagram

DIRECTIONS: A Venn Diagram consists of three large intersecting circles that are used to compare and contrast three different but related objects, concepts, or events. A Venn diagram is useful when researching a topic that requires comparison and contrast. As you conduct the research, look for interrelationships among subtopics. Record areas of commonality in the intersecting segments of the circles, and record differences in the appropriate non-intersecting segments of the circles.

See page 53 for reproducible copy.

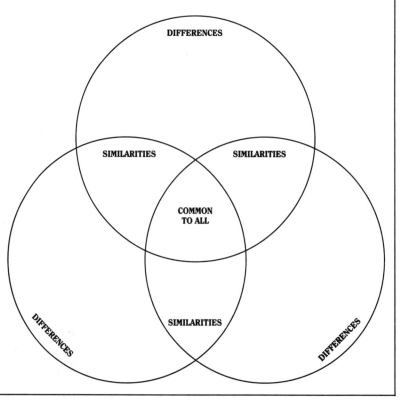

The ABC's of Science

A _____

B _____

C _____

D _____

E _____

F _____

G _____

H _____

I _____

J _____

K _____

L _____

M _____

N _____

O _____

P _____

Q _____

R _____

S _____

T _____

U _____

V _____

W _____

X _____

Y _____

Z _____

*Standards-Based SCIENCE Graphic Organizers, Rubrics,
and Writing Prompts for Middle Grade Students*

Attribute Grid

Science Topic: _____

Attributes, Characteristics, Qualities, Criteria															
Objects, Events, Places, Things															

Standards-Based SCIENCE Graphic Organizers, Rubrics, and Writing Prompts for Middle Grade Students

Biographical Sketch of a Scientist

Name of Scientist:

Date/Place of Birth and Date/Place of Death:

Early Childhood Experiences:

Adult Life Experiences:

Personal Character Traits/Skills/Interests/Strengths:

Important Discoveries/Contributions:

Problems/Difficulties Encountered and Overcome:

Special Awards/Celebrations/Tributes:

Cause/Effect Fishbone Map

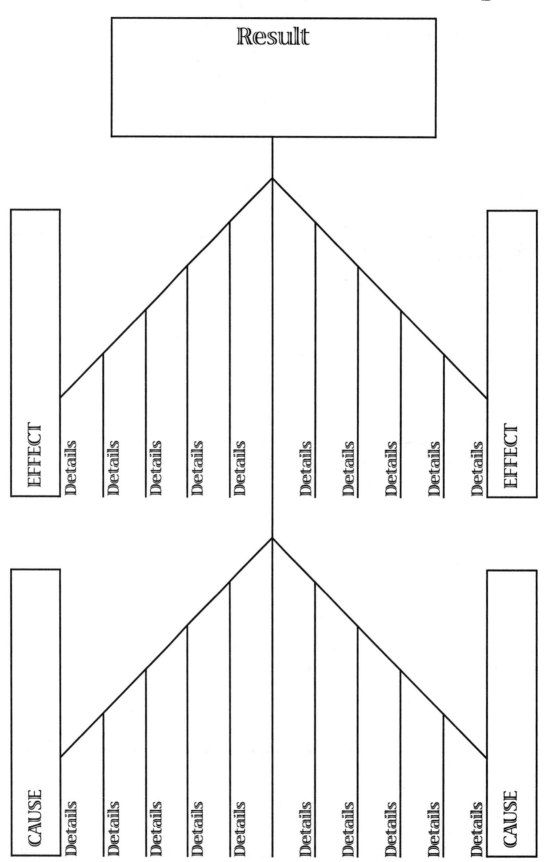

Result

EFFECT — Details Details Details Details Details | Details Details Details Details Details — EFFECT

CAUSE — Details Details Details Details Details | Details Details Details Details Details — CAUSE

Charting Science Skills

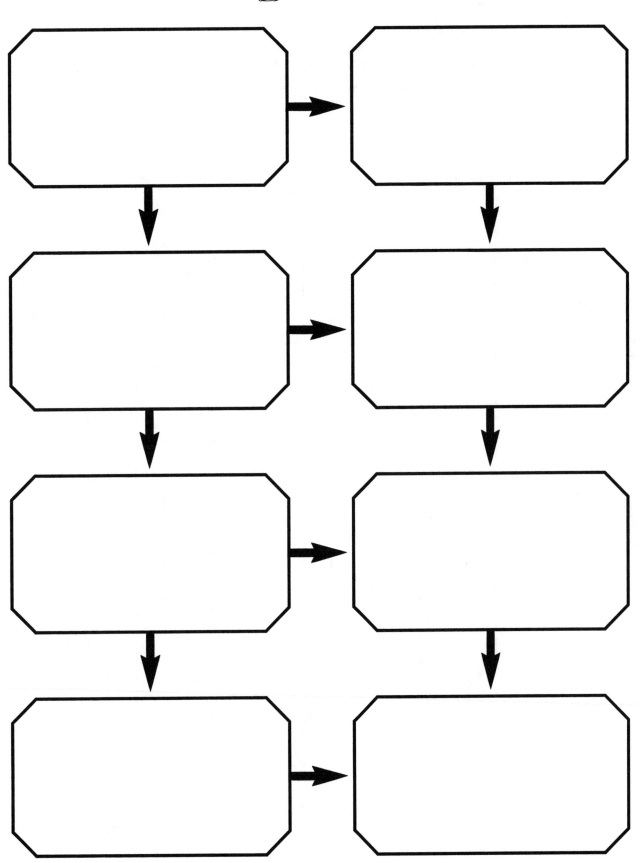

29

A Concept Builder

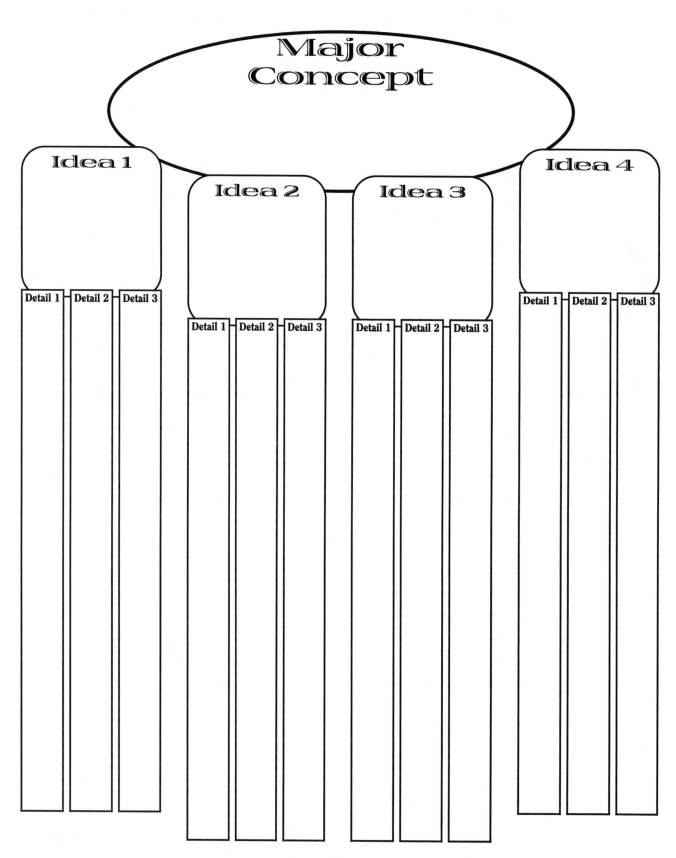

Standards-Based SCIENCE Graphic Organizers, Rubrics, and Writing Prompts for Middle Grade Students

The Cycle Graph

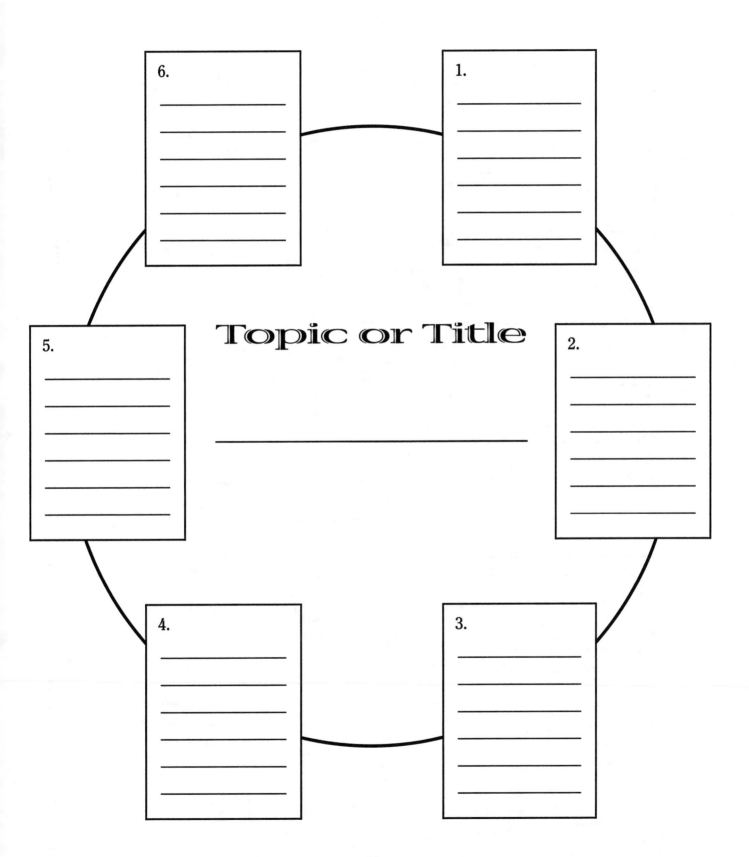

6.

1.

5.

Topic or Title

2.

4.

3.

Discussion Guide

1. What are five facts that you learned about the topic that you are willing to share?

Fact One:

Fact Two:

Fact Three:

Fact Four:

Fact Five:

2. What do you find most interesting about the subject?

3. What confuses you about the subject?

4. What else would you like to know about the subject?

5. How do you suppose scientists originally found out about this topic?

6. If you could ask the experts about the topic, what would you ask them?

7. What are some new pieces of information that you have learned on this topic as a result of this discussion? Write these on the back of this sheet of paper.

Event/Outcome Graph

	Event 1	Event 2	Event 3	Event 4	Event 5	Event 6
Result						
Result						
Result						
Result						
Result						
Result						

*Standards-Based SCIENCE Graphic Organizers, Rubrics,
and Writing Prompts for Middle Grade Students*

Fact, Comment, and Question
Textbook Survey

Fact
Comment/Reaction/Opinion
Question

Fact
Comment/Reaction/Opinion
Question

Fact
Comment/Reaction/Opinion
Question

5 W's and How of Scientific Theories, Principles, and Laws

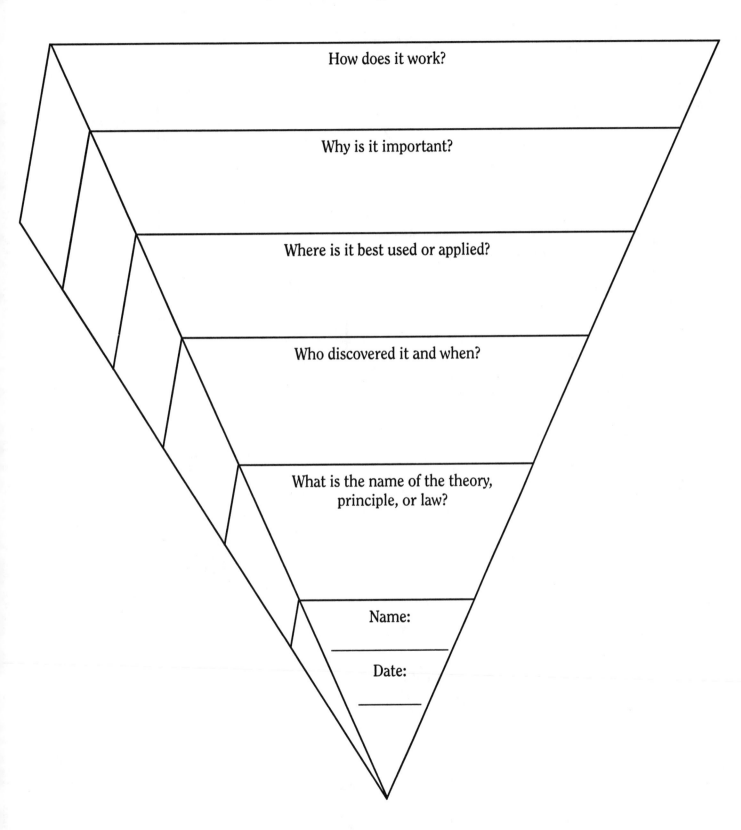

How does it work?

Why is it important?

Where is it best used or applied?

Who discovered it and when?

What is the name of the theory, principle, or law?

Name:

_____

Date:

_____

*Standards-Based SCIENCE Graphic Organizers, Rubrics,
and Writing Prompts for Middle Grade Students*

Flowcharting

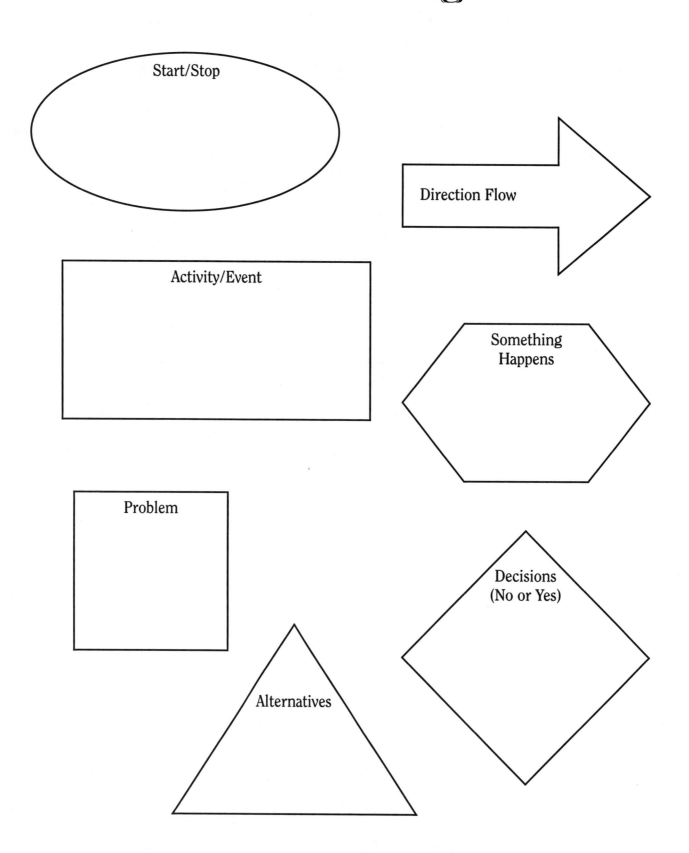

Hypothesis-Proof-Opinion Chart

Hypothesis/Proof/Opinion Chart

Hypothesis:	Proof Statements:

Opinion/Proof Notes and Conclusion

Idea Organizer

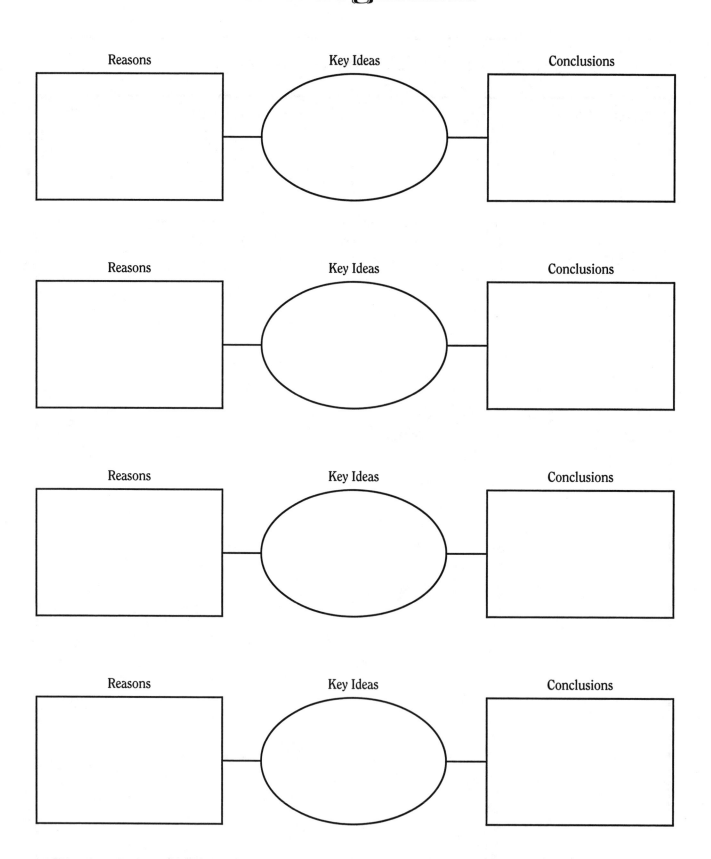

Reasons   Key Ideas   Conclusions

Reasons   Key Ideas   Conclusions

Reasons   Key Ideas   Conclusions

Reasons   Key Ideas   Conclusions

Standards-Based SCIENCE Graphic Organizers, Rubrics, and Writing Prompts for Middle Grade Students

Investigating Significant Event
Step By Step

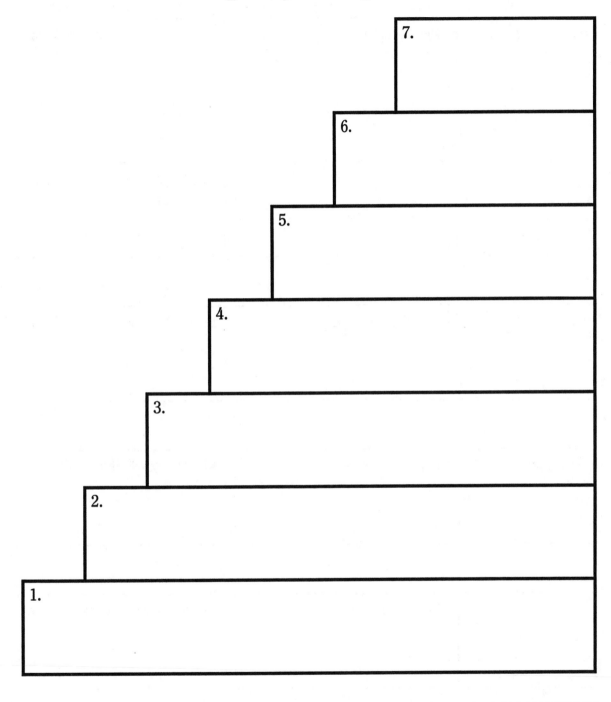

Statement/Conclusion/Commentary:

*Standards-Based SCIENCE Graphic Organizers, Rubrics,
and Writing Prompts for Middle Grade Students*

Log of Scientific Terms

Scientific Term	Definition of Term	Illustration/Sentence of Term
Scientific Term	Definition of Term	Illustration/Sentence of Term
Scientific Term	Definition of Term	Illustration/Sentence of Term
Scientific Term	Definition of Term	Illustration/Sentence of Term
Scientific Term	Definition of Term	Illustration/Sentence of Term
Scientific Term	Definition of Term	Illustration/Sentence of Term

Standards-Based SCIENCE Graphic Organizers, Rubrics, and Writing Prompts for Middle Grade Students

Panel Planner

Topic for Panel _____

Name of Panel Moderator _____

Question 1: _____

Question 2: _____

Question 3: _____

Question 4: _____

Panel Member One

_____

_____

Panel Member Two

_____

_____

Panel Member Three

_____

_____

Panel Member Four

_____

_____

Standards-Based SCIENCE Graphic Organizers, Rubrics,
and Writing Prompts for Middle Grade Students

Picture/Graph Response Sheet

Describe what you see.

Explain what is happening.

Tell why this is happening.

Give reasons why it was chosen for this book.

Position Paper Planner

Introductory Paragraph

1. Eye-catching example, startling statement, personal anecdote, dramatic quotation, unusual data/fact to catch reader's attention.

2. Thesis Statement

Body Paragraph One

1. Topic Sentence

    2. Supporting Sentence

    3. Supporting Sentence

    4. Supporting Sentence

Body Paragraph Two

1. Topic Sentence

    2. Supporting Sentence

    3. Supporting Sentence

    4. Supporting Sentence

Body Paragraph Three

1. Topic Sentence

    2. Supporting Sentence

    3. Supporting Sentence

    4. Supporting Sentence

Concluding Paragraph

1. Concluding sentence based on thesis statement.

2. Final statement in form of rhetorical question, point to ponder, or basis for further study.

Standards-Based SCIENCE Graphic Organizers, Rubrics, and Writing Prompts for Middle Grade Students

Problem-Solving Tree

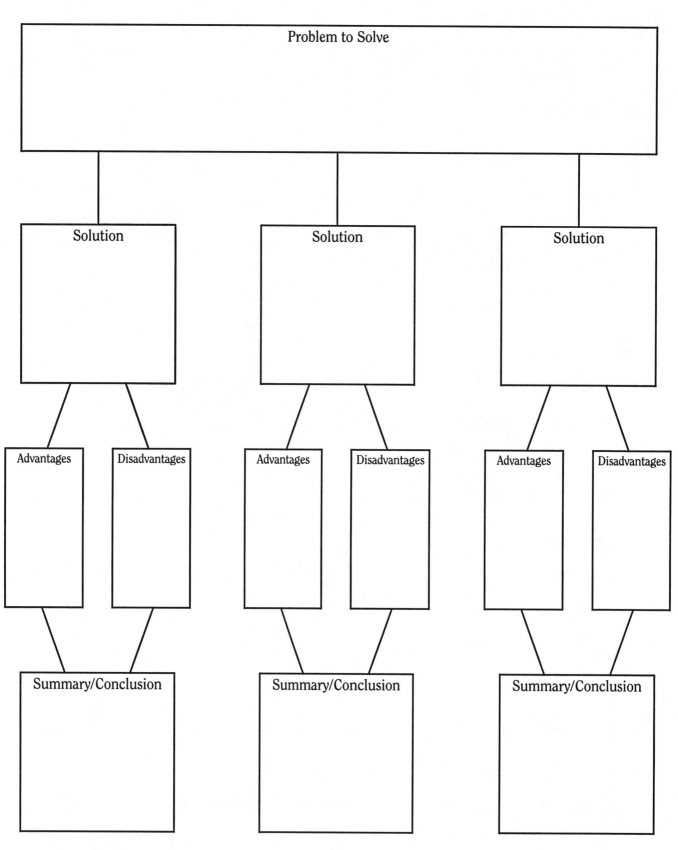

Problem to Solve

Solution

Solution

Solution

Advantages

Disadvantages

Advantages

Disadvantages

Advantages

Disadvantages

Summary/Conclusion

Summary/Conclusion

Summary/Conclusion

Standards-Based SCIENCE Graphic Organizers, Rubrics, and Writing Prompts for Middle Grade Students

Report Outline
Using Bloom's Taxonomy

KNOWLEDGE:
List all of the important facts you have found about your topic.

COMPREHENSION:
Explain, summarize, describe, or give examples to elaborate on your topic.

APPLICATION:
Demonstrate or construct something related to your topic.

ANALYSIS:
Compare and contrast two things about your topic.

SYNTHESIS:
Make a prediction about or combine ideas on your topic in a new and useful way.

EVALUATION:
Do a plus and minus chart on your topic and draw a set of defensible conclusions based on the findings presented in the chart.

Standards-Based SCIENCE Graphic Organizers, Rubrics, and Writing Prompts for Middle Grade Students

The Research Regulator

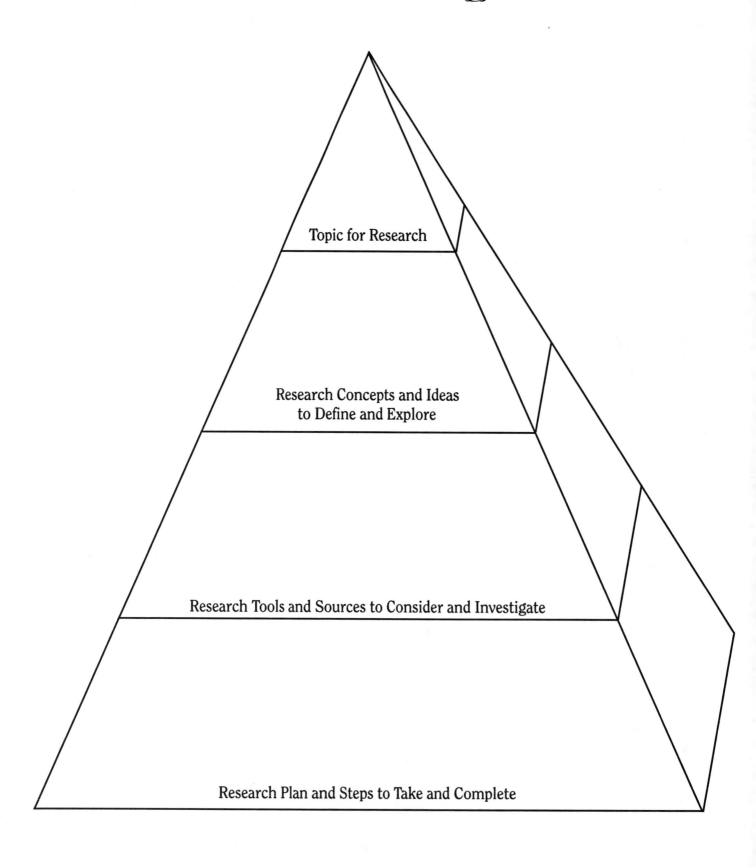

Topic for Research

Research Concepts and Ideas
to Define and Explore

Research Tools and Sources to Consider and Investigate

Research Plan and Steps to Take and Complete

Scientific Categories
and Their Relationships

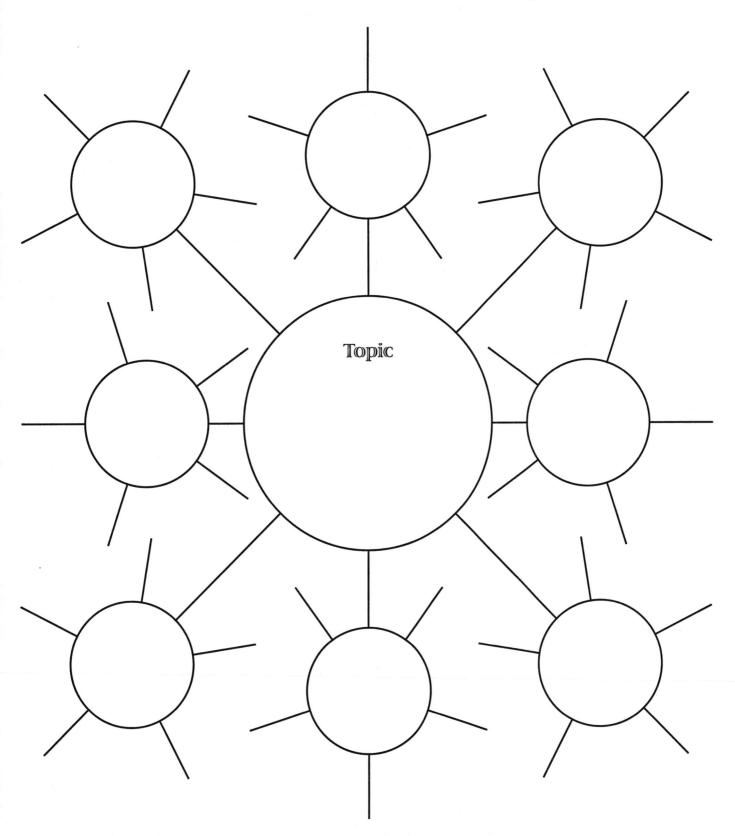

Topic

*Standards-Based SCIENCE Graphic Organizers, Rubrics,
and Writing Prompts for Middle Grade Students*

Storyboard

1.	6.
2.	7.
3.	8.
4.	9.
5.	10.

Standards-Based SCIENCE Graphic Organizers, Rubrics,
and Writing Prompts for Middle Grade Students

Copyright ©2001 by Incentive Publications, Inc.
Nashville, TN.

Time Line Template

Topic:	Dates	Events	Notes or Comments

*Standards-Based SCIENCE Graphic Organizers, Rubrics,
and Writing Prompts for Middle Grade Students*

Tools of Science

1. Microscope _____

2. Telescope _____

3. Thermometer _____

4. Meter Stick _____

5. Electric Circuit _____

6. Magnet _____

7. Pulley _____

8. Periodic Table _____

9. Beaufort Scale _____

10. Mohs' Scale _____

11. Weather Vane _____

12. Bunsen Burner _____

13. Balance Scale _____

14. Prism _____

15. Beaker or Flask _____

16. Magnifying Glass _____

17. Inclined Plane _____

18. Litmus Paper _____

19. Tuning Fork _____

Using Multiple Intelligences to Gather Data for Science Project or Presentation

1. Verbal/Linguistic Intelligence:
   What books, magazines, newspapers, and other print materials are available for you to review?

   _____

   _____

   _____

   _____

2. Logical/Mathematical Intelligence:
   How can charts, graphs, diagrams, and technology tools help you gather information?

   _____

   _____

   _____

   _____

3. Visual/Spatial Intelligence:
   What pictures, photographs, maps, videos, posters, and other forms of visuals have information about the topic?

   _____

   _____

   _____

   _____

4. Musical/Rhythmic Intelligence:
   How might songs, raps, and audio tapes relate to your topic?

   _____

   _____

   _____

   _____

Standards-Based SCIENCE Graphic Organizers, Rubrics, and Writing Prompts for Middle Grade Students

Using Multiple Intelligences to Gather Data for Science Project or Presentation
(continued)

5. Bodily-Kinesthetic Intelligence:
   What computer software, Internet web sites, skits, dances, or physical/sporting events could serve you as reliable resources?

   _____

   _____

   _____

   _____

6. Interpersonal Intelligence:
   What family members, friends, teachers, experts, or community groups/organizations/ institutions are there for you to interview in person, by telephone, or through chat rooms?

   _____

   _____

   _____

   _____

7. Intrapersonal Intelligence:
   What personal experiences, readings, feelings, opinions, or ideas do you have on the topic that you can pull from?

   _____

   _____

   _____

   _____

8. Naturalist Intelligence:
   How do Mother Nature and wildlife relate to your topic?

   _____

   _____

   _____

   _____

Venn Diagram

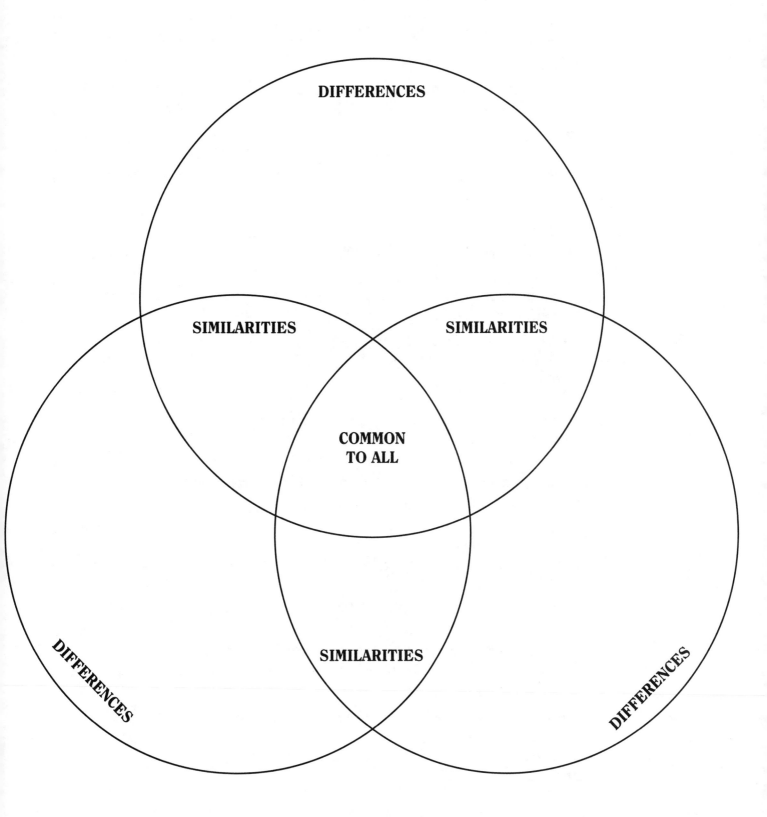

DIFFERENCES

SIMILARITIES   **SIMILARITIES**

**COMMON
TO ALL**

DIFFERENCES

SIMILARITIES

DIFFERENCES

*Standards-Based SCIENCE Graphic Organizers, Rubrics,
and Writing Prompts for Middle Grade Students*

Questions for Teachers and Students to Consider About Using Graphic Organizers in the Classroom

1. What is a graphic organizer and what types of graphic organizers are best for my subject area?

2. How can I use graphic organizers to help students collect information, make interpretations, draw conclusions, solve problems, outline plans, and become better reflective thinkers?

3. What graphic organizers can I use that are hierarchical structures with levels and subsets?

4. What graphic organizers can I use that are conceptual structures which take a central idea or concept and branch out from it?

5. What graphic organizers can I use that are sequential structures that focus on the order, chronology, or flow of ideas?

6. What graphic organizers can I use that are cyclical structures, which form a pattern in a circular format?

7. How can I model the use of graphic organizers with my students before introducing them into the instructional process?

8. How can I best model the use of graphic organizers with a wall chart, an overhead projector, or a drawing on the chalkboard?

9. How do graphic organizers show and explain relationships between content and sub-content and how do they in turn relate to the other content areas?

10. How can graphic organizers be considered teaching tools for all types of learners?

11. How can graphic organizers be used as assessment tools to show a student's understanding of a concept and a student's way of thinking about that concept?

12. How do graphic organizers support Bloom's Taxonomy and the Multiple Intelligences?

13. Are graphic organizers best used with individual students or can they be part of cooperative learning group tasks?

14. How can students use graphic organizers to assess their own learning?

Standards-Based SCIENCE Graphic Organizers, Rubrics, and Writing Prompts for Middle Grade Students

Copyright ©2001 by Incentive Publications, Inc. Nashville, TN.

Writing Prompts

It has been said that science values systems, order, and organization. Give scientific examples to show that this is true.

_____
_____
_____
_____
_____
_____
_____

Design a simple experiment to show the transfer of energy from one object to another using items commonly found in the kitchen. Draw a series of diagrams to explain your experiment.

_____
_____
_____
_____
_____
_____
_____
_____

Do you think the space program is important? Should we keep sending rockets, satellites, and people into space? Explain.

_____
_____
_____
_____
_____
_____
_____
_____

GUIDELINES
FOR USING WRITING PROMPTS

PURPOSE

A journal is: a collection of ideas, thoughts, and opinions; a place to outline papers and projects, a place to record observations about something read, written or discussed, a record keeping tool, a place in which to write personal reactions or responses, a reference file to help a student monitor individual growth, a way for students to dialogue with teachers and peers, a place for a student to write about a variety of topics, and a place for reflections on learned material.

FORMATS

Several formats are available for students working with journal writing. Some of the most appealing formats to students and teachers are: special notebooks, segments of audiotapes, file cards, and handmade diaries.

WRITING TIME

There are several approaches students may use in timing their journal writing. Some may write daily for five minutes, semi-weekly for ten minutes, weekly for fifteen minutes, or write as inspiration strikes.

STUDENT FEEDBACK

There are several methods, both formal and informal, for sharing students' journal work. Choose one or more of the following to implement in your classroom.
1) Students share their journal entries with their peers.
2) Students read journal entries aloud to the class on a volunteer basis.
3) Journals may be used for "conferencing."
4) Journals are to be taken home and shared with parents or guardians.
5) Students may analyze and answer one of their own journal entries one or more days after entry was recorded to acknowledge personal changes in perspective.

Standards-Based SCIENCE Graphic Organizers, Rubrics, and Writing Prompts for Middle Grade Students

Copyright ©2001 by Incentive Publications, Inc. Nashville, TN.

It has been said that science values systems, order, and organization. Give scientific examples to show that this is true.

_____

_____

_____

_____

_____

_____

_____

_____

_____

_____

Use this starter statement as the beginning of a paragraph about the world of science: Science is . . .

_____

_____

_____

_____

_____

_____

_____

_____

_____

_____

_____

Standards-Based SCIENCE Graphic Organizers, Rubrics,
and Writing Prompts for Middle Grade Students

In your own words, explain the concept of *evolution*. To get started, consider this question: How do things evolve?

_____

_____

_____

_____

_____

_____

_____

_____

_____

Science requires a multitude of explanations to describe things that happen in the world. Think of a scientific phenomenon that has always fascinated you and explain it so that a young child could understand it.

_____

_____

_____

_____

_____

_____

_____

_____

_____

_____

Standards-Based SCIENCE Graphic Organizers, Rubrics, and Writing Prompts for Middle Grade Students

Cite scientific evidence that *form* and *function* go together. Which comes first?

_____

_____

_____

_____

_____

_____

_____

_____

_____

_____

If you were asked to locate a book in each of the following categories, what would you look for and how might each be used: science book, science fiction book, science textbook, and science reference book.

_____

_____

_____

_____

_____

_____

_____

_____

_____

Scientists classify items according to their similarities or likenesses. Devise a system of classifying workers in your community, people in your neighborhood, or students in your school. Be sure to develop a set of groups or categories and criteria for placement of individuals in those groups. Finally, list the members of each group.

_____

_____

_____

_____

_____

_____

_____

_____

_____

Select a science theory that has changed over time. Draw a series of pictures to show these various changes.

_____

_____

_____

_____

_____

_____

_____

_____

_____

_____

Create your own definition of science inquiry.

_____

_____

_____

_____

_____

_____

_____

_____

_____

_____

Explain what is meant by the "scientific method." Can this method be used in other subject areas as well as science? Give reasons for your answer.

_____

_____

_____

_____

_____

_____

_____

_____

_____

_____

Standards-Based SCIENCE Graphic Organizers, Rubrics, and Writing Prompts for Middle Grade Students

Scientists make discoveries through the act of inquiry. Name an important discovery that you hope scientists will make in the near future and give three good reasons for your choice.

_____

_____

_____

_____

_____

_____

_____

_____

_____

_____

_____

Imagine that you have been chosen to receive the prestigious Nobel prize for science. Describe what wonderful thing you have accomplished through your ability to do scientific inquiry.

_____

_____

_____

_____

_____

_____

_____

_____

_____

_____

Standards-Based SCIENCE Graphic Organizers, Rubrics, and Writing Prompts for Middle Grade Students

Why do you think it is difficult to be a scientist? What special skills, talents, qualities, and experiences would you need to be an expert in this occupation?

_____

_____

_____

_____

_____

_____

_____

_____

_____

_____

Create a colorful and descriptive flyer that would inform parents about the exciting things that go on in your science class or programs.

_____

_____

_____

_____

_____

_____

_____

_____

_____

_____

Standards-Based SCIENCE Graphic Organizers, Rubrics,
and Writing Prompts for Middle Grade Students

List ten different topics from your science textbook that fall into the category of physical science. Rank order these from your most favorite to your least favorite, and give reasons for your first and last choices.

_____

_____

_____

_____

_____

_____

_____

_____

_____

_____

_____

How would your life be different if the force of gravity disappeared while you were getting ready for school in the morning or ready for bed at night?

_____

_____

_____

_____

_____

_____

_____

_____

_____

_____

Design a simple experiment to show the transfer of energy from one object to another using items commonly found in the kitchen. Draw a series of diagrams to explain your experiment.

_____

_____

_____

_____

_____

_____

_____

_____

_____

In your own words, explain why our world continues to suffer from energy shortages even though we have multiple energy sources throughout the world.

_____

_____

_____

_____

_____

_____

_____

_____

_____

_____

*Standards-Based SCIENCE Graphic Organizers, Rubrics,
and Writing Prompts for Middle Grade Students*

Locate at least five different sites on the Internet that would be good virtual field trips for a project in physical science. Develop an annotated bibliography for each site.

_____

_____

_____

_____

_____

_____

_____

_____

_____

_____

Create a Rube Goldberg invention that capitalizes on motions and forces to make something happen.

_____

_____

_____

_____

_____

_____

_____

_____

_____

Standards-Based SCIENCE Graphic Organizers, Rubrics, and Writing Prompts for Middle Grade Students

Write about a physical science area or topic in which you would like to be an expert.

_____

_____

_____

_____

_____

_____

_____

_____

_____

_____

Create a logo or slogan for each of the following types of scientists (biologists) who study living things: botanist (plants), zoologist (animals), cytologist (cells), entomologist (insects), herpetologist (reptiles and amphibians), ichthyologist (fish), mammalogist (mammals), and ornithologist (birds).

_____

_____

_____

_____

_____

_____

_____

_____

_____

_____

Visualize a trip inside the human body. What would you see and do?

_____

_____

_____

_____

_____

_____

_____

_____

_____

_____

Define "cycle" and give examples of at least three different cycles that occur in nature.

_____

_____

_____

_____

_____

_____

_____

_____

_____

_____

Standards-Based SCIENCE Graphic Organizers, Rubrics,
and Writing Prompts for Middle Grade Students

List ten scientific terms that are related to a topic in life science. For each term, write down a definition that makes sense to you.

_____

_____

_____

_____

_____

_____

_____

_____

_____

_____

_____

Make a list of some adaptations that occur in nature that you consider to be very unusual or unique. Apply one or more of these to people and speculate how they would enable human beings to better live in their environment.

_____

_____

_____

_____

_____

_____

_____

_____

_____

_____

_____

Standards-Based SCIENCE Graphic Organizers, Rubrics,
and Writing Prompts for Middle Grade Students

Defend or negate this statement: It is okay for scientists to experiment on animals because they lead to practices and discoveries that can eventually save human lives.

_____

_____

_____

_____

_____

_____

_____

_____

_____

_____

_____

Write about the types of animals you would study if you were a naturalist.

_____

_____

_____

_____

_____

_____

_____

_____

_____

_____

_____

Standards-Based SCIENCE Graphic Organizers, Rubrics, and Writing Prompts for Middle Grade Students

Plan a special celebration for Earth Day in your school. What special ideas do you have for publicity, for student activities, for refreshments, and for fun?

_____

_____

_____

_____

_____

_____

_____

_____

_____

_____

Explain your views on the success or lack of success of recycling efforts at the local, state, and national levels.

_____

_____

_____

_____

_____

_____

_____

_____

_____

_____

If you could design a billboard to express how you feel about saving the earth and its resources in your community, what would it say and what would it show?

_____

_____

_____

_____

_____

_____

_____

_____

_____

_____

Create an instruction book for preserving and conserving the earth that could be distributed to families in your school.

_____

_____

_____

_____

_____

_____

_____

_____

_____

Standards-Based SCIENCE Graphic Organizers, Rubrics, and Writing Prompts for Middle Grade Students

Prepare a set of entries that would reflect what you would most likely see and do while visiting each of these regions of the world: deserts, tropics, mountains, tundra, and plains.

_____

_____

_____

_____

_____

_____

_____

_____

_____

_____

_____

Write a story at least half a page long using the word "earth" or "space" as many times as you can.

_____

_____

_____

_____

_____

_____

_____

_____

_____

_____

_____

In the song, "America the Beautiful," one reads the words: "Oh, beautiful for spacious skies, for amber waves of grain." What parts of the earth do you think are being described here? Think of some songs you know that would make a good national anthem for your country because they describe the beauties and features of the earth.

_____

_____

_____

_____

_____

_____

_____

_____

_____

_____

Write about something you have always wanted to know more about when it comes to technological design.

_____

_____

_____

_____

_____

_____

_____

_____

_____

_____

Standards-Based SCIENCE Graphic Organizers, Rubrics, and Writing Prompts for Middle Grade Students

Do you think the space program is important? Should we keep sending rockets, satellites, and people into space? Explain.

_____

_____

_____

_____

_____

_____

_____

_____

_____

_____

Generate a list of jobs related to the world of technology that did not exist 50 years ago. Can you think of one for most letters of the alphabet?

_____

_____

_____

_____

_____

_____

_____

_____

_____

_____

*Standards-Based SCIENCE Graphic Organizers, Rubrics,
and Writing Prompts for Middle Grade Students*

Discuss the many ways that technology has improved our lives and ways that it has actually complicated our lives when it comes to the field of science.

_____

_____

_____

_____

_____

_____

_____

_____

_____

_____

Would you want to be part of a design team that investigates new ways to infuse technology into our everyday lives? Why or why not?

_____

_____

_____

_____

_____

_____

_____

_____

_____

_____

Standards-Based SCIENCE Graphic Organizers, Rubrics, and Writing Prompts for Middle Grade Students

Explain ways that technology and science have influenced or changed the work of law enforcement workers and criminal investigators.

_____

_____

_____

_____

_____

_____

_____

_____

_____

_____

Many people think that Bill Gates is one of the most powerful and innovative leaders in our technological world today. How do you feel about his leadership status and Microsoft contributions?

_____

_____

_____

_____

_____

_____

_____

_____

_____

_____

Write about something you should do right now to improve your personal health or fitness.

_____

_____

_____

_____

_____

_____

_____

_____

_____

_____

_____

Explain how you feel when you see someone litter or pollute the environment. Give specific examples to support your observations and emotions.

_____

_____

_____

_____

_____

_____

_____

_____

_____

_____

_____

_____

Standards-Based SCIENCE Graphic Organizers, Rubrics, and Writing Prompts for Middle Grade Students

What natural hazards do you encounter in your environment on a weekly, monthly, or yearly basis and what can you do or are you doing about them?

_____

_____

_____

_____

_____

_____

_____

_____

_____

_____

Discuss some things you have done to help the environment or to conserve natural resources.

_____

_____

_____

_____

_____

_____

_____

_____

_____

*Standards-Based SCIENCE Graphic Organizers, Rubrics,
and Writing Prompts for Middle Grade Students*

Describe the risks and benefits of mandated organ donor programs, of legal life support systems, and of potential euthanasia or mercy killings all made possible today because of science and technology efforts.

_____

_____

_____

_____

_____

_____

_____

_____

_____

Think about what you would teach your students about science and technology if you were the science teacher for a day.

_____

_____

_____

_____

_____

_____

_____

_____

_____

Standards-Based SCIENCE Graphic Organizers, Rubrics,
and Writing Prompts for Middle Grade Students

Record several sentences about what governments need to know about you and your life before they pass legislation on personal health issues, hazards, and risks related to children and adolescents.

_____

_____

_____

_____

_____

_____

_____

_____

_____

_____

_____

Discuss ways that science is related to other subject areas such as mathematics, social studies, physical education, and personal health.

_____

_____

_____

_____

_____

_____

_____

_____

_____

_____

_____

Standards-Based SCIENCE Graphic Organizers, Rubrics, and Writing Prompts for Middle Grade Students

It has been said that science is a human endeavor. What do you think this means?

_____

_____

_____

_____

_____

_____

_____

_____

_____

_____

Write about a scientific discovery that has occurred or that you would like to see occur in your lifetime.

_____

_____

_____

_____

_____

_____

_____

_____

_____

_____

_____

Compose a comprehensive paragraph describing a scientist from history that you have admired or studied from the past.

_____

_____

_____

_____

_____

_____

_____

_____

_____

_____

_____

Describe something you would like to examine or study in a science lab.

_____

_____

_____

_____

_____

_____

_____

_____

_____

_____

What could you teach yourself about the nature or history of science that might make a difference in how you see things or how you feel about things?

_____

_____

_____

_____

_____

_____

_____

_____

_____

_____

Based on your studies in science to date, explain what you would do with $100 million dollars if you were to donate it to expand one's understanding of the world of science and technology and/or the world of science from one's personal and social perspective.

_____

_____

_____

_____

_____

_____

_____

_____

_____

Look out of your classroom window. Think about what scientific phenomena your science classes have allowed you to "see." List as many principles of science as you can "see" out of the window.

_____

_____

_____

_____

_____

_____

_____

_____

_____

_____

What scientific principle remains a mystery to you? What is it about this concept that is difficult to understand? List the questions you would like to have answered to solve this mystery.

_____

_____

_____

_____

_____

_____

_____

_____

_____

_____

Standards-Based SCIENCE Graphic Organizers, Rubrics, and Writing Prompts for Middle Grade Students

1. How can I fit journals into my particular discipline and classroom schedule?

2. How do I know if journals will work with my students or my subject area?

3. How can I coordinate journals with my team members and their classes?

4. What materials will I need to begin the use of journals?

5. How will I introduce the concept of journals to my students?

6. What kinds of reactions and responses can I expect from my students in their journal entries?

7. How can I get a sense of ownership or interest by students with journal prompts in my classroom?

8. How will I find time to reply to their journals, and what kind of responses should I write?

9. How can I overcome student resistance or misunderstanding of the journal concept?

10. How can I use journals for assessment purposes, and what kinds of information am I likely to receive from them?

11. How should I review or evaluate journals, and how will I keep track of this process?

12. How do I grade journal entries?

Rubrics

Guidelines
FOR USING RUBRICS

1. Agree on a definition of a rubric and its importance to the evaluation process. The purpose of a rubric is to answer the question: "What are the conditions of success and to what degree are those conditions met by the student involved in a specific learning task?"

2. Effective rubrics reflect the most important elements of an assigned task, product, or performance and they enable both student and teacher to accurately depict the level of competence or stage of development of that student.

3. Effective rubrics encourage student self-evaluations and, in fact, are shared with students prior to beginning the task so that students know exactly what represents quality work.

4. Rubrics are designed to explain more concretely what a child knows and can do and are less subjective than other means of student evaluation.

5. Every rubric must have two components which are: (1) characteristics or criteria for quality work on a specific task and (2) determination of the specific levels of proficiency or degrees of success for each part of a task.

6. A holistic rubric consists of paragraphs arranged in a hierarchy so that each level of proficiency has a paragraph describing factors that would result in that specific level.

7. An analytic rubric consists of a listing of criteria most characteristic of that task accompanied with the degrees of success for each model listed separately beside or under each criterion.

8. Before implementing rubrics in a discipline, it is important to define and discuss the elements of a quality performance in that discipline and to collect samples of rubrics as models for scrutiny and potential application.

Standards-Based SCIENCE Graphic Organizers, Rubrics, and Writing Prompts for Middle Grade Students

Copyright ©2001 by Incentive Publications, Inc.
Nashville, TN.

9. Before implementing rubrics in a discipline, study samples of student work to determine realistic attributes common to varied performances at different levels of proficiency. Translate these attributes into descriptors for the degrees of proficiency and then establish a rating scale to delineate those degrees of proficiency.

10. Avoid using generalities such as *good, better, little, none,* or *somewhat* in your rating scales; quantify and qualify in more specific terms. Construct analytical rubrics with four to six degrees of proficiency for each criterion. Then, weight each criterion to determine the percentage or number of points each is worth.

11. Distribute and discuss any rubric directly with the student before he or she embarks on the assigned product or performance task. Encourage the student to set personal goals for their desired level of accomplishment on each criterion. Insist that students revise their work if it does not meet minimum expectations on any criterion of the task.

12. When introducing rubrics to students, start out by collaboratively constructing a rubric for a fun class event such as planning a party, structuring a field trip, or designing a contest.

13. Remember that to be most effective as an important component of science programs, rubrics must be accompanied by carefully planned opportunities for meta-cognitive reflections throughout the assessment experience. While rubrics are comprised of checklists containing sets of criteria for measuring the elements of product, performance, or portfolio, the meta-cognitive reflections provide for self-assessment observations completely unique to the students' own learning goals, expectations, and experiences.

14. The use of rubrics can augment, reinforce, personalize, and strengthen but not replace the assessment program mandated by curriculum guidelines or system requirements. As with any well-balanced assessment program the master teacher or teaching team will continue to take full advantage of all tools, strategies, and techniques available to construct and make use of a balanced assessment program to meet individual needs.

Assessment Checklist for The Physical World: Matter

Rating Scale: ✔+   ✔   ✔−

1. Student is able to identify and define these terms:

Matter	Rating: _____	Weight	Rating: _____
States of Matter	Rating: _____	Inertia	Rating: _____
Mass	Rating: _____	Density	Rating: _____

2. Student is able to explain these laws:

Law of conservation of mass   Rating: _____

Law of conservation of energy   Rating: _____

Law of conservation of mass-energy   Rating: _____

3. Student is able to identify and define these terms:

Atom	Rating: _____	Electron	Rating: _____
Solution	Rating: _____	Base	Rating: _____
Nucleus	Rating: _____	Element	Rating: _____
Compound	Rating: _____	Chemical change	Rating: _____
Proton	Rating: _____	Atomic number	Rating: _____
Molecule	Rating: _____	Physical change	Rating: _____
Neutron	Rating: _____	Mixture	Rating: _____
Acid	Rating: _____	pH scale	Rating: _____

4. Student is able to describe and explain the organization of the Periodic Table of Elements.   Rating: _____

5. Student is able to demonstrate understanding of chemistry as the science of matter.   Rating: _____

6. Additional concepts student has learned:

_____

_____

_____

Assessment Checklist for The Physical World: Energy, Motion, and Work

Rating Scale:　　✔+　　　　　　✔　　　　　　✔−

---

1. **Student is able to identify and define these terms:**

Energy	**Rating:** _____	Force	**Rating:** _____
Potential energy	**Rating:** _____	Newton	**Rating:** _____
Kinetic energy	**Rating:** _____	Joules (J)	**Rating:** _____
Work	**Rating:** _____	Motion	**Rating:** _____

---

2. **Student is able to explain and give examples of Newton's Laws:**

   The First Law of Motion　　　　　　　　　　　　　**Rating:** _____

   The Second Law of Motion　　　　　　　　　　　　**Rating:** _____

   The Third Law of Motion　　　　　　　　　　　　　**Rating:** _____

---

3. **Student is able to state and apply the formulas for both measuring the amount of work done and the speed of work referred to as power.**　　　**Rating:** _____

---

4. **Student is able to explain and give examples of the concept of *mechanical advantage*.**　　　**Rating:** _____

---

5. **Student is able to identify and demonstrate understanding of these simple machines and combinations of these simple machines (complex machines):**

Pulley	**Rating:** _____	Inclined plane	**Rating:** _____
Wheel and axle	**Rating:** _____	Screw	**Rating:** _____
Lever	**Rating:** _____	Wedge	**Rating:** _____

---

6. **Additional concepts student has learned:**

   _____

   _____

   _____

   _____

Assessment Checklist for The Physical World: Light and Sound

Rating Scale: ✔+ ✔ ✔−

---

1. **Student is able to identify and define these terms:**

Light	**Rating:** _____	Wavelengths	**Rating:** _____
Photons	**Rating:** _____	Spectrum	**Rating:** _____
Reflection	**Rating:** _____	Prism	**Rating:** _____
Refraction	**Rating:** _____		

---

2. **Student is able to distinguish between reflection of light and refraction of light.**   **Rating:** _____

---

3. **Student is able to explain the Law of Reflection and its angle of incidence (I).**   **Rating:** _____

---

4. **Student is able to identify and define these terms:**

Sound	**Rating:** _____	Intensity of sound (sound level)	**Rating:** _____
Vibrations	**Rating:** _____	Decibels	**Rating:** _____
Compression waves	**Rating:** _____	Sound barrier	**Rating:** _____
Expansion waves	**Rating:** _____	Sonic boom	**Rating:** _____
Amplitude	**Rating:** _____	Echoes	**Rating:** _____
Frequency	**Rating:** _____	Reverberation	**Rating:** _____
Pitch	**Rating:** _____	Hertz (Hz)	**Rating:** _____

---

5. **Student is able to discuss the speed of sound and its relationship to the speed of light.**   **Rating:** _____

---

6. **Student is able to construct a simple chart to show how noise is measured in decibels and how some common sounds measure up.**   **Rating:** _____

---

7. **Additional concepts student has learned:**

   _____

   _____

   _____

Assessment Checklist for
The Physical World:
Magnetism and Electricity

Rating Scale: ✔+   ✔   ✔−

---

1. **Student is able to identify and define these terms:**

   Electricity   **Rating:** _____   Circuit   **Rating:** _____
   Electrons   **Rating:** _____   Alternating currents   **Rating:** _____
   Static electricity **Rating:** _____   Direct currents   **Rating:** _____
   Conductor   **Rating:** _____   Magnets and magnetism   **Rating:** _____

---

2. **Student is able to construct a closed circuit.**   **Rating:** _____

---

3. **Student is able to explain how a battery works.**   **Rating:** _____

---

4. **Student is able to relate the following terms to the measurement of electricity and to one another:**

   Amperes   **Rating:** _____   Ohms   **Rating:** _____
   Volts   **Rating:** _____   Watts   **Rating:** _____

---

5. **Student is able to state and explain Ohm's Law.**   **Rating:** _____

---

6. **Student is able to identify different types of magnets and to locate their magnetic poles.**   **Rating:** _____

---

7. **Student is able to demonstrate the use of a compass.**   **Rating:** _____

---

8. **Student is able to describe the connection between magnetism and electricity.**   **Rating:** _____

---

9. **Student is able to explain how a galvanometer is used to measure electric current.**   **Rating:** _____

---

10. **Additional concepts student has learned:**

    _____

    _____

    _____

Assessment Checklist for the Physical World: Heat & Temperature

Rating Scale: ✔+   ✔   ✔−

---

1. Student is able to identify and define these terms:

Heat   **Rating:** _____   Celsius   **Rating:** _____
Temperature   **Rating:** _____   Degree   **Rating:** _____
Calorie   **Rating:** _____   Galileo's
Fahrenheit   **Rating:** _____   Thermometer   **Rating:** _____

**2. Student is able to convert temperatures
from the Fahrenheit to the Celsius scale and vice versa.**   **Rating:** _____

**3. Student is able to state and explain
the Three Laws of Thermodynamics.**   **Rating:** _____

**4. Student is able to explain the relationship
between calories and body weight.**   **Rating:** _____

**5. Student is able to explain how heat causes
both physical and chemical changes.**   **Rating:** _____

**6. Student is able to describe how heat flows from warmer to cooler bodies in
the following ways:**

Radiation   **Rating:** _____
Conduction   **Rating:** _____
Convection   **Rating:** _____

---

7. Additional concepts student has learned:

_____

_____

_____

_____

Assessment Checklist for Life Science: The Animal Kingdom

Rating Scale: ✔+   ✔   ✔−

---

1. Student is able to identify and define these terms:

Kingdoms	**Rating:** _____	Carnivores	**Rating:** _____
Organism	**Rating:** _____	Herbivores	**Rating:** _____
Microorganism	**Rating:** _____	Omnivores	**Rating:** _____
Vertebrate	**Rating:** _____	Predators	**Rating:** _____
Invertebrate	**Rating:** _____	Scavengers	**Rating:** _____
Cold-blooded	**Rating:** _____	Insectivores	**Rating:** _____
Warm-blooded	**Rating:** _____	Animal cell	**Rating:** _____

---

2. Student is able to classify living things according to system, order, and organization that includes these eight categories:

Kingdom	**Rating:** _____	Order	**Rating:** _____
Phylum	**Rating:** _____	Family	**Rating:** _____
Subphylum	**Rating:** _____	Genus	**Rating:** _____
Class	**Rating:** _____	Species	**Rating:** _____

---

3. Student is able to identify, define, and give examples of the following invertebrates:

Sponges	**Rating:** _____	Mollusks	**Rating:** _____
Stinging-cell Animals	**Rating:** _____	Sea Stars and their Relatives	**Rating:** _____
Flatworms	**Rating:** _____	Arthropods	**Rating:** _____
Roundworms	**Rating:** _____	Metamorphosis	**Rating:** _____
Segmented Worms	**Rating:** _____		

---

4. Student is able to identify, define, and give examples of the following vertebrates:

Fish	**Rating:** _____	Birds	**Rating:** _____
Amphibians	**Rating:** _____	Mammals	**Rating:** _____
Reptiles	**Rating:** _____		

Standards-Based SCIENCE Graphic Organizers, Rubrics, and Writing Prompts for Middle Grade Students

5. Student is able to explain how various animals reproduce. Rating: _____

6. Student is able to identify, define, and give examples of these five kingdoms:

Animals	Rating: _____	Protists	Rating: _____
Plants	Rating: _____	Monerans	Rating: _____
Fungi	Rating: _____		

7. Student is able to distinguish between diurnal and nocturnal animals. Rating: _____

8. Student is able to relate these concepts to animal behavior:

Adaptation	Rating: _____	Migration	Rating: _____
Camouflage	Rating: _____	Hibernation	Rating: _____

9. Other concepts and content learned:

_____

_____

_____

_____

_____

_____

Student Comments:

_____

_____

_____

Teacher Comments:

_____

_____

_____

Standards-Based SCIENCE Graphic Organizers, Rubrics, and Writing Prompts for Middle Grade Students

Assessment Checklist for Life Science: The Plant Kingdom

Rating Scale: ✔+   ✔   ✔—

---

1. **Student is able to identify and give examples of seed plants and plants that do not make seeds.**   **Rating:** _____

---

2. **Student is able to identify and define these terms related to seed plants:**

Gymnosperm	**Rating:** _____	Conifer	**Rating:** _____
Monocot	**Rating:** _____	Cotyledon	**Rating:** _____
Dicot	**Rating:** _____		

---

3. **Student is able to identify and summarize the importance of the three main parts of a plant including the appropriate use of these concepts:**

Photosynthesis	**Rating:** _____	Transpiration	**Rating:** _____
Chlorophyll	**Rating:** _____	Capillary action	**Rating:** _____
Respiration	**Rating:** _____	Life cycle	**Rating:** _____

---

4. **Student is able to explain how plants reproduce by seeds using these concepts in the explanations:**

Germination	**Rating:** _____	Pollination	**Rating:** _____
Fertilization	**Rating:** _____		

---

5. **Student is able to explain how plants reproduce without seeds.**   **Rating:** _____

---

6. **Student is able to identify and define these main parts of a flower:**

Petal	**Rating:** _____	Sepal	**Rating:** _____
Stamen (anther and filament)	**Rating:** _____	Stigma	**Rating:** _____
		Pollen tube	**Rating:** _____
Pistil	**Rating:** _____	Ovary	**Rating:** _____

---

7. **Other content and concepts learned:**

_____

_____

_____

Standards-Based SCIENCE Graphic Organizers, Rubrics, and Writing Prompts for Middle Grade Students

Assessment Checklist for Life Science: Ecology

Rating Scale: ✔+   ✔   ✔−

---

1. Student is able to identify, describe, and give examples of these biomes:

Grasslands	**Rating:** _____	Tundra	**Rating:** _____
Deserts	**Rating:** _____	Coniferous Forests	**Rating:** _____
Scrublands	**Rating:** _____	Tropical Rain Forests	**Rating:** _____
Deciduous Forests	**Rating:** _____		

---

2. Student is able to define the concepts of *ecology* and *ecosystem*.   **Rating:** _____

---

3. Student is able to define, explain, and give examples of food chains and food webs using these concepts:

Producers	**Rating:** _____	Decomposers	**Rating:** _____
Consumers	**Rating:** _____		

---

4. Student is able to define, explain, and give examples of natural cycles, including:

Water cycle	**Rating:** _____	Carbon and	
Nitrogen cycle	**Rating:** _____	oxygen cycle	**Rating:** _____

---

5. Student is able to discuss each of these environmental and conservation issues:

Endangered species	**Rating:** _____	Thermal pollution	**Rating:** _____
Land pollution	**Rating:** _____	Global warming and	
Noise pollution	**Rating:** _____	Greenhouse Effect	**Rating:** _____
Air pollution	**Rating:** _____		

---

6. Other concepts and content learned:

_____

_____

_____

Assessment Checklist for Earth/Space Science: Planet Earth and the Land

Rating Scale: ✔+   ✔   ✔−

---

1. Student is able to identify and define these terms:

Earth's crust	**Rating:** _____	Tectonic plates	**Rating:** _____
Earth's mantle	**Rating:** _____	Continental drift	**Rating:** _____
Earth's core, inner core, outer core	**Rating:** _____	Eras of geologic time	**Rating:** _____

---

2. Student is able to explain how these types of rocks are formed, and give examples of each:

Igneous rocks	**Rating:** _____	Metamorphic rocks	**Rating:** _____
Sedimentary rocks	**Rating:** _____		

---

3. Student is able to identify and give examples of common minerals using Mohs' Scale.   **Rating:** _____

---

4. Student is able to identify and define these four types of soil:

Clay	**Rating:** _____	Sand	**Rating:** _____
Silt	**Rating:** _____	Loam	**Rating:** _____

---

5. Student is able to describe, give examples, and explain about these landforms:

Mountains	**Rating:** _____	Plains	**Rating:** _____
Hills	**Rating:** _____	Plateaus	**Rating:** _____
Valleys	**Rating:** _____		

---

6. Student is able to describe, give examples, and explain these natural events that shape the land:

Earthquakes	**Rating:** _____	Volcanoes and volcanic eruptions	**Rating:** _____

Standards-Based SCIENCE Graphic Organizers, Rubrics, and Writing Prompts for Middle Grade Students

7. Student is able to differentiate between these bodies of water:

Oceans	Rating: _____	Bays	Rating: _____
Seas	Rating: _____	Rivers	Rating: _____
Gulfs	Rating: _____	Lakes	Rating: _____

8. Student is able explain each of the following concepts in some detail:

Ocean floor	Rating: _____	Ocean waves	Rating: _____
Ocean zones	Rating: _____	Ocean tides	Rating: _____
Ocean currents	Rating: _____		

9. Student is able to describe the two forms of glaciers and how glaciers are formed.   **Rating:** _____

10. Additional concepts student has learned:

_____

_____

_____

_____

_____

_____

_____

_____

_____

_____

_____

_____

_____

_____

_____

_____

_____

_____

Standards-Based SCIENCE Graphic Organizers, Rubrics, and Writing Prompts for Middle Grade Students

Assessment Checklist for Earth/Space Science: The Atmosphere and Weather/Climate

Rating Scale: ✔+   ✔   ✔−

1. **The student will be able to identify and define the following atmospheric concepts:**

Atmosphere	**Rating:** _____	Stratosphere	**Rating:** _____
Exosphere	**Rating:** _____	Troposphere	**Rating:** _____
Thermosphere	**Rating:** _____	Atmospheric	
Mesosphere	**Rating:** _____	pressure	**Rating:** _____

2. **The student will be able to identify and define the following weather/climate-related concepts:**

Weather	**Rating:** _____	Wind & wind patterns	**Rating:** _____
Climate	**Rating:** _____	Beaufort scale	**Rating:** _____
Air mass	**Rating:** _____	Hail, sleet, snow	**Rating:** _____
Air temperature	**Rating:** _____	Thunderstorms	**Rating:** _____
Atmospheric pressure	**Rating:** _____	Cyclones	**Rating:** _____
Dew point	**Rating:** _____	Thunderstorms	**Rating:** _____
Fog	**Rating:** _____	Tornadoes	**Rating:** _____
Front	**Rating:** _____	Typhoons	**Rating:** _____
Humidity	**Rating:** _____	Hurricanes	**Rating:** _____
Precipitation	**Rating:** _____		

3. **The student will be able to explain how the seasons of the year are determined including the use of these concepts:**

Tropics	**Rating:** _____	Rotations	**Rating:** _____
Poles	**Rating:** _____	Axis	**Rating:** _____
Temperate zones	**Rating:** _____	Northern hemisphere	**Rating:** _____
Equator	**Rating:** _____	Southern hemisphere	**Rating:** _____
Orbits	**Rating:** _____		

Standards-Based SCIENCE Graphic Organizers, Rubrics, and Writing Prompts for Middle Grade Students

4. Additional concepts student has learned:

_____

_____

_____

_____

_____

_____

_____

_____

_____

_____

_____

Student Comments:

_____

_____

_____

_____

_____

_____

Teacher Comments:

_____

_____

_____

_____

_____

_____

Standards-Based SCIENCE Graphic Organizers, Rubrics, and Writing Prompts for Middle Grade Students

Assessment Checklist for Earth/Space Science: Outer Space

Rating Scale: ✔+   ✔   ✔−

---

1. The student will identify and define the following star/galaxy concepts:

Universe	**Rating:** _____	Novas and Supernovas	**Rating:** _____
Astronomy	**Rating:** _____	Black holes	**Rating:** _____
Star	**Rating:** _____	Dying stars	**Rating:** _____
Giants and Super giants	**Rating:** _____	Neutron stars	**Rating:** _____
Dwarfs	**Rating:** _____	Pulsars	**Rating:** _____
Variable stars	**Rating:** _____	Quasars	**Rating:** _____
Star clusters	**Rating:** _____	Galaxies	**Rating:** _____
Double stars	**Rating:** _____	Big Bang Theory	**Rating:** _____

2. The student will identify and define each of these concepts related to the Solar System:

Sun	**Rating:** _____	Comets	**Rating:** _____
Planets	**Rating:** _____	Asteroids	**Rating:** _____
Moons	**Rating:** _____	Meteors	**Rating:** _____

3. The student will describe each of these planets in terms of:

- substance
- rings
- distance from Sun
- moons
- diameter

- length of day and year
- gravity compared to earth
- atmosphere
- temperature
- weight of object

Mercury	**Rating:** _____	Saturn	**Rating:** _____
Venus	**Rating:** _____	Uranus	**Rating:** _____
Earth	**Rating:** _____	Neptune	**Rating:** _____
Mars	**Rating:** _____	Pluto	**Rating:** _____
Jupiter	**Rating:** _____		

Standards-Based SCIENCE Graphic Organizers, Rubrics, and Writing Prompts for Middle Grade Students

4. The student will demonstrate understanding of each of these concepts:

Solar eclipse   **Rating:** _____   Lunar eclipse   **Rating:** _____

Phases of the moon   **Rating:** _____

5. The student will demonstrate understanding of the need for space exploration as well as some familiarity with the chronology of space exploration over the past two decades.   **Rating:** _____

6. Additional concepts student has learned:

_____

_____

_____

_____

_____

_____

_____

_____

_____

_____

_____

Student Comments:

_____

_____

_____

Teacher Comments:

_____

_____

_____

Standards-Based SCIENCE Graphic Organizers, Rubrics, and Writing Prompts for Middle Grade Students

Scoring Rubric for Responding to Writing Prompts

DIRECTIONS: Use this rubric to score selected entries into a journal, diary, or learning log using predetermined science prompts either provided by the teacher or generated by the student.

Score 3: Student . . .

- Understands purpose and expected outcomes of writing prompt.

- Has no difficulty in responding to writing prompt.

- Produces quality ideas, examples, information, and evidence in response to writing prompt.

- Uses writing skills of grammar, punctuation, and spelling that add to reader's understanding and interest in ideas and content presented.

Score 2: Student . . .

- Shows partial understanding of purpose and expected outcomes of writing prompt.

- Has some difficulty in responding to writing prompt.

- Produces a few quality ideas, examples, information, and evidence in response to writing prompt.

- Uses writing skills of grammar, punctuation, and spelling that do not inhibit the reader's understanding and interest in ideas and content presented.

Score 1: Student . . .

- Does not understand purpose and expected outcomes of writing prompt.

- Is not able to respond to prompt.

- Lacks sufficient background of ideas, examples, information, and evidence to relate to prompt.

- Uses writing skills of grammar, punctuation, and spelling that inhibits the reader's understanding and interest in ideas and content presented.

Student Comments:

_____

_____

Teacher Comments:

_____

_____

Generic Rubric for Science Assignment or Task

DIRECTIONS: Use this generic outline to design a comprehensive rubric that could be used to assess the quality of a science assignment or task. Be sure to list at least four criteria or expected outcomes under each category and make certain that all criteria/outcomes are related for each of the scores given.

Score Six: Exemplary Achievement ____

1.   3.
2.   4.

Score Five: Commendable Achievement ____

1.   3.
2.   4.

Score Four: Adequate Achievement ____

1.   3.
2.   4.

Score Three: Some Evidence of Achievement ____

1.   3.
2.   4.

Score Two: Limited Evidence of Achievement ____

1.   3.
2.   4.

Score One: Minimal Evidence of Achievement ____

1.   3.
2.   4.

Score Zero: No Response ____

Additional notes:

_____

_____

_____

Assessment Rubric for Science Experiment/Lab Report

Rating Scale

①　　　　　②　　　　　③　　　　　④　　　　　⑤

Throwing Tomatoes　　　　**Round of Applause**　　　　**Standing Ovation**

1. I started with a hypothesis for conducting my experiment.	Rating: _____
2. I gathered the necessary materials and equipment.	Rating: _____
3. I applied the scientific method step-by-step.	Rating: _____
4. I got the results I expected or understand why they were different.	Rating: _____
5. I wrote up a comprehensive and accurate lab report describing my experiment and its findings.	Rating: _____
6. My experiment was successful in terms of design, process, and lab report.	Rating: _____

The most interesting thing about this experiment for me was:

_____

_____

A result that surprised me was:

_____

_____

Something I would do differently next time if I were to repeat this design would be:

_____

_____

Assessment for
Chalkboard Presentation
(Chalk Talk)
on Scientific Law,
Theory, or Principle

Rating Scale: 0 = Not evident   2 = Evident

1 = Slightly evident   3 = Very evident

1. Appropriateness of Topic

I selected a scientific law, theory, or principle of interest
to others and myself.   **Rating:** _____

2. Appropriateness of Topic to Chalk Talk

I selected a scientific law, theory, or principle that lends itself
to a chalkboard explanation, diagram, or drawing.   **Rating:** _____

3. Quality of Content in Chalk Talk

The content of my chalk talk was presented according to
a logical scope and sequence of ideas and information.   **Rating:** _____

4. Coordination of Script and Graphics

The script for my chalk talk was developed and presented in coordination
with the graphics drawn to illustrate the ideas in the script.   **Rating:** _____

5. Clarity and Delivery of Oral Speaking Skills

I used a good speaking voice and enunciated my words clearly
in the oral delivery of my chalk talk presentation.   **Rating:** _____

6. Graphics/Creativity

The information and graphics for my chalk talk
were creatively organized and delivered.   **Rating:** _____

7. Time Constraints

The chalk talk was appropriate in terms of
the time specified for the presentation.   **Rating:** _____

Assessment for Science-Based Problem Solving Role Play or Demonstration Skit

1. Student chooses an appropriate science-based problem, topic, or situation for role play or skit.	Hot! 1	Warm 2	Lukewarm 3	Tepid 4	Cold 5
2. Student shows maturity in selecting classmates to play other characters in role play or skit.	Hot! 1	Warm 2	Lukewarm 3	Tepid 4	Cold 5
3. Student demonstrates knowledge of science concepts in writing script for role play or skit.	Hot! 1	Warm 2	Lukewarm 3	Tepid 4	Cold 5
4. Student writes good dialogue in communicating scientific information for role play or skit.	Hot! 1	Warm 2	Lukewarm 3	Tepid 4	Cold 5
5. Student demonstrates quality group skills in orchestrating role play or skit.	Hot! 1	Warm 2	Lukewarm 3	Tepid 4	Cold 5
6. Student adequately rehearses role play or skit.	Hot! 1	Warm 2	Lukewarm 3	Tepid 4	Cold 5
7. Student and group present and perform role play or skit well.	Hot! 1	Warm 2	Lukewarm 3	Tepid 4	Cold 5
8. Student successfully conveys accurate and interesting scientific information to the audience.	Hot! 1	Warm 2	Lukewarm 3	Tepid 4	Cold 5

Standards-Based SCIENCE Graphic Organizers, Rubrics, and Writing Prompts for Middle Grade Students

Assessment Rubric for Scientific Problem Solving

	Rating Scale		
	Accomplished	**So-So**	**Needs Work**
1. Student works well without direction.			
2. Student manages time effectively.			
3. Student recognizes problem to be solved.			
4. Student asks good questions to define problem.			
5. Student accurately defines problem.			
6. Student formulates and states hypothesis correctly.			
7. Student successfully plans procedure to test hypothesis.			
8. Student adequately collects, records, and tabulates data.			
9. Student organizes data in meaningful way.			
10. Student shows interest and commitment throughout the process.			

Student Comments:

_____

_____

_____

Teacher Comments:

_____

_____

_____

Assessment Rubric for Independent Study Contract

Steps I followed in completing my independent study contract.

1. I selected a science topic that I felt was appropriate and manageable for this contract purpose.

   First Base   Second Base   Third Base   Home Run!

2. I met with my teacher to talk about the topic and my ideas for the study project and received approval to proceed with the contract. Together we designed the format of the contract and agreed on the terms of the contract.

   First Base   Second Base   Third Base   Home Run!

3. I developed a comprehensive outline, time line, and action plan to implement the specifications of the contract.

   First Base   Second Base   Third Base   Home Run!

4. I met regularly with the teacher to give updates on my progress and to solicit constructive suggestions and alternative solutions to any problems that occurred.

   First Base   Second Base   Third Base   Home Run!

5. I successfully completed the terms of the independent study contract.

   First Base   Second Base   Third Base   Home Run!

6. I had a final meeting with the teacher to reflect on the results of my project and to evaluate both its strengths and those things that could be improved next time.

   First Base   Second Base   Third Base   Home Run!

7. I enjoyed working on my independent study contract and would enjoy doing another one sometime in the future.

   First Base   Second Base   Third Base   Home Run!

Standards-Based SCIENCE Graphic Organizers, Rubrics, and Writing Prompts for Middle Grade Students

Assessment Rubric for
A Student-Led Conference

Rating Scale   0 = Not observed   2 = Tell me what I need to improve!
                    1 = Tell me what I am doing wrong.   3 = I'm doing terrific!

---

1. **I established a specific time, date, and place for the conference with both my teacher(s) and my parents/guardians.**   Rating: _____

2. **I prepared a formal agenda for the conference using input from all participants in attendance.**   Rating: _____

3. **I conducted the conference with guidance from my teacher(s).**   Rating: _____

4. **I prepared a portfolio of personal science artifacts (assignments) that represented all-important areas of our science program.**   Rating: _____

5. **I shared personal reflections on most (or all) of the artifacts in my portfolio.**   Rating: _____

6. **I was able to give satisfactory answers to questions generated at the conference.**   Rating: _____

7. **I enjoyed conducting the conference.**   Rating: _____

8. **I learned something important about myself as a result of this conference.**   Rating: _____

Parent/Guardian Reactions:

_____

_____

Teacher Reactions:

_____

_____

Assessment Rubric for Group Research Project & Presentation

Rating Scale: ★ ★ ★ ★ ★ ★ ★ ★ ★ ★

1. The topic we chose for our science project was appropriate and of interest to all group members.	Rating: _____
2. We first discussed the topic as a group to determine what we already knew about it.	Rating: _____
3. We collectively developed an outline and a time line for conducting more research on the topic.	Rating: _____
4. We divided the areas for research among all group members.	Rating: _____
5. After completing our research, we met to synthesize the information into a single report, assigning responsibilities for writing different sections, editing content, and proofing drafts.	Rating: _____
6. We divided the report into sections for presenting the information orally to the class.	Rating: _____
7. We rehearsed our presentation focusing on eye contact, body language, and clear speaking.	Rating: _____
8. Where appropriate, we included visuals and props in our presentation for clarity and interest.	Rating: _____

Comments:

_____

_____

_____

Assessment Rubric for Science Fair Project or Exhibit

1. Appropriateness of Topic

My topic was well chosen in terms of its content or substance, its interest to others, its timeliness, and availability of information.

Out of the Gate   Home Stretch
          Second Lap

2. Quality of Planning Process

I developed a detailed outline, time line, and action plan for its successful completion.

Out of the Gate   Home Stretch
          Second Lap

3. Acceptability of Resources

My resources for research and gathering data were varied and extensive.

Out of the Gate   Home Stretch
          Second Lap

4. Graphics/Creativity

I demonstrated creativity in its overall design, format, and presentation.

Out of the Gate   Home Stretch
          Second Lap

5. Quality of Expected Outcomes

My findings and results were clear and well-documented.

Out of the Gate   Home Stretch
          Second Lap

6. Application of Scientific Process

My ability to use and apply the scientific process was evident throughout the project or exhibit.

Out of the Gate   Home Stretch
          Second Lap

Notes to myself:

_____

_____

_____

_____

Standards-Based SCIENCE Graphic Organizers, Rubrics, and Writing Prompts for Middle Grade Students

Copyright ©2001 by Incentive Publications, Inc. Nashville, TN.

Cooperative Learning
Group Performance

Topic: _____

Group Members: _____

_____

_____

_____

Date: _____ **Reporter:** _____

Rating Scale: 3 = Outstanding   2 = Satisfactory   1 = Needs Improvement

Rating:

	Rating
1. Each member of the group contributed ideas and suggestions for setting goals, assigning roles, and developing and carrying out a plan of action.	
2. Each member of our group carried out the duties of his or her role.	
3. Each member of our group exhibited respect for the other members.	
4. Each member of our group exhibited good listening skills and an interest in other group members' contributions.	
5. Each member of the group applied conflict resolution skills as appropriate.	
6. Each member of the group contributed to the content focus and overall performance.	
7. A positive, pleasant, and cheerful atmosphere was maintained during group meetings.	
8. Group goals were achieved.	
9. The overall rating we would give our group is . . .	

*Standards-Based SCIENCE Graphic Organizers, Rubrics,
and Writing Prompts for Middle Grade Students*

Assessment Rubric for Using Bloom's Taxonomy to Evaluate a Product, Performance, or Portfolio

Type of Product: _____

Topic: _____

Knowledge: Evidence of learned facts, methods, procedures, or concepts.

_____	_____	_____
Great Evidence	Ample Evidence	Little Evidence

Comprehension: Evidence of understanding of facts, methods, procedures, or concepts.

_____	_____	_____
Great Evidence	Ample Evidence	Little Evidence

Application: Evidence of use of the information in new situations.

_____	_____	_____
Great Evidence	Ample Evidence	Little Evidence

Analysis: Evidence of analysis, recognition of assumptions, and evaluation of relevancy of information.

_____	_____	_____
Great Evidence	Ample Evidence	Little Evidence

Synthesis: Evidence of putting information together in a new and creative way.

_____	_____	_____
Great Evidence	Ample Evidence	Little Evidence

Evaluation: Evidence of acceptance or rejection of information on the basis of criteria.

_____	_____	_____
Great Evidence	Ample Evidence	Little Evidence

Comments by Student: _____

_____

_____

Signed _____ Date _____

Comments by Teacher: _____

_____

_____

Signed _____ Date _____

Assessment Rubric for Evaluating Quality of Reference and Research Resources

Check the type of reference and research resource you are using for this assessment purpose:

_____ Internet web site   _____ Magazine/journal article   _____ Movie

_____ Encyclopedia   _____ Interview with expert   _____ Slides

_____ Reference book   _____ Site visitation   _____ Historical document

_____ Newspaper article   _____ Video or audio tape   _____ Photographs

_____ Other _____

1. Availability

Is the source easy to access and readily available?

Yes   Somewhat   No

2. Authority

Is the author, expert, or individual who is providing the source of information qualified?

Yes   Somewhat   No

3. Appropriateness

Is the source relevant and directly related to the information you need?

Yes   Somewhat   No

4. Currency

Is the information source timely, up-to-date, and accurate?

Yes   Somewhat   No

5. Suitability

Is the information translatable by you and understandable to you?

Yes   Somewhat   No

6. Reliability

Is the information based on fact and valid opinions?

Yes   Somewhat   No

Questions for Teachers and Students to Consider About
Using **Rubrics** in the Classroom

1. What is a rubric and what kinds of rubrics are there?
   _____

2. What are some characteristics of effective rubrics?
   _____

3. What are the critical components in the design of rubrics?
   _____

4. What is a holistic rubric?
   _____

5. What is an analytical rubric?
   _____

6. Are rubrics developed by students, by teachers, or both?
   _____

7. How does one decide on the criteria of a given rubric?
   _____

8. How does one determine the best type of rating scale for a given rubric?
   _____

9. Are rubrics appropriate for all types of instruction and all types of content areas?
   _____

10. How does one teach students to use and value rubrics as an assessment tool?
    _____

11. Why are rubrics an effective way to measure student performance?
    _____

12. Are rubrics appropriate for measuring the quality of a student-generated product?
    _____

13. How does one translate the results of a rubric into a numerical grade?
    _____

14. How does one use rubrics to guide evaluation and establish a shared standard of quality work?
    _____

15. Are the development and use of rubrics more time consuming for students and teachers as an assessment tool and, if so, is that time commitment worth the effort?
    _____

Standards-Based SCIENCE Graphic Organizers, Rubrics, and Writing Prompts for Middle Grade Students

Appendix

National Academy of Sciences Standards

Planning Matrix

Criteria for Creating Your Own Rubric

Performance, Project, or Task Independent Study Contract

Judging Criteria for a Science Fair Project

Bloom's Taxonomy of Cognitive Thinking Skills for Students

Outline for Developing A Unit on Any Science Topic

Experiment Form for Use with Any Science Topic

Bibliography

Index

National Academy of Sciences Standards

Unifying Concepts and Processes

As a result of activities in grades 5-8, all students should develop understanding and abilities aligned with the following concepts: systems, order, and organization; evidence, models, and explanation; constancy, change, and measurement; evolution and equilibrium; and form and function.

Science as Inquiry

As a result of activities in grades 5-8, all students should develop: abilities necessary to do scientific inquiry and understandings about scientific inquiry.

Physical Science

As a result of their activities in grades 5-8, all students should develop an understanding of: properties and changes of properties in matter, motions and force, and transfer of energy.

Life Science

As a result of their activities in grades 5-8, all students should develop an understanding of: structure and function in living systems, reproduction and heredity, regulations and behavior, populations and ecosystems, and diversity and adaptations of organisms.

Standards-Based SCIENCE Graphic Organizers, Rubrics, and Writing Prompts for Middle Grade Students

Earth and Space Science

As a result of their activities in grades 5-8, all students should develop an understanding of: structure of the Earth system, Earth's history, and Earth in the solar system.

Science and Technology

As a result of their activities in grades 5-8, all students should develop: abilities of technological design and understandings about science and technology.

Science in Personal and Social Perspectives

As a result of their activities in grades 5-8, all students should develop understandings of: personal health, populations, resources, and environments, natural hazards, risks and benefits, and science and technology in society.

History and Nature of Science

As a result of activities in grades 5-8, all students should develop understanding of: science as human endeavor, nature of science, and history of science.

Reprinted with permission from *National Science Education Standards*. Copyright 1996 by the National Academy of Sciences. Courtesy of the National Academy Press, Washington, D.C.

*Standards-Based SCIENCE Graphic Organizers, Rubrics,
and Writing Prompts for Middle Grade Students*

Planning Matrix

Correlatives: National Science Standards as Identified by the National Academy of Sciences with activities and projects in Standards-Based Graphic Organizers, Rubrics, and Writing Prompts, Incentive Publications, 2001.

Standards	Graphic Organizers	Writing Prompts	Rubrics	Reinforcement & Reflection
Life Science	25, 26, 27, 28, 29, 30, 31, 34, 35, 36, 37, 40, 42, 45, 47, 48, 49, 50, 53	67, 68, 69, 70	95, 96, 97, 98, 105, 106, 107, 108, 109, 114, 116	10, 56, 58, 86, 88, 89, 118, 120, 126, 127, 128, 129, 130, 131, 133, 134, 135, 136, 137
Earth and Space Science	25, 26, 27, 28, 29, 30, 31, 34, 35, 36, 37, 40, 42, 45, 47, 48, 49, 50, 53	71, 72, 73, 74	99, 100, 101, 102, 103, 104, 105, 106, 107, 108, 109, 114, 116	10, 56, 58, 86, 88, 89, 118, 121, 126, 127, 128, 129, 130, 131, 133, 134, 135, 136, 137
Science and Technology	26, 28, 30, 32, 33, 36, 37, 38, 39, 40, 41, 43, 44, 45, 47, 48, 49, 50, 51, 52, 53	75, 76, 77, 78	105, 106, 107, 109, 113, 114, 116	10, 56, 58, 86, 88, 89, 113, 115, 118, 121, 126, 127, 128, 129, 130, 131, 133, 134, 135, 136, 137
Unifying Concepts and Processes	28, 30, 32, 33, 35, 41, 43, 44, 47, 48, 49, 51, 52, 53	57, 58, 59	105, 106, 107, 108, 109, 110, 116	10, 56, 58, 86, 118, 120, 124, 125, 126, 127, 128, 129, 130, 131, 133, 134, 135, 136, 137

Standards-Based SCIENCE Graphic Organizers, Rubrics, and Writing Prompts for Middle Grade Students

Planning Matrix

Correlatives: National Science Standards as Identified by the National Academy of Sciences with activities and projects in Standards-Based Graphic Organizers, Rubrics, and Writing Prompts, Incentive Publications, 2001.

Standards	Graphic Organizers	Writing Prompts	Rubrics	Reinforcement & Reflection
Science as Inquiry	32, 33, 37, 38, 39, 41, 43, 44, 45, 46, 48, 49, 51, 52	60, 61, 62	105, 106, 107, 108, 109, 110, 111, 113, 114, 116, 117	10, 56, 58, 86, 112, 113, 115, 118, 120, 124, 125, 126, 127, 128, 129, 130, 131, 133, 134, 135, 136, 137
Physical Science	25, 26, 27, 28, 29, 30, 34, 35, 36, 37, 40, 42, 45, 47, 48, 49, 50, 53	63, 64, 65, 66	90, 91, 92, 93, 94, 105, 106, 107, 108, 109, 114, 116	10, 56, 58, 86, 118, 120, 124, 125, 126, 127, 128, 129, 130, 131, 132, 133, 134, 135, 136, 137
Science in Personal and Social Perspectives	26, 28, 29, 32, 33, 37, 38, 39, 41, 43, 44, 45, 46, 47, 48, 49, 51, 52, 53	79, 80, 81, 82	105, 106, 107, 109, 110, 111, 113, 114, 116, 117	10, 56, 58, 86, 88, 89, 112, 113, 118, 121, 124, 125, 126, 127, 128, 129, 130, 131, 133, 134, 135, 136
History and Nature of Science	12, 26, 27, 30, 32, 33, 38, 39, 41, 43, 45, 46, 48, 49, 51, 52	83, 84, 85	105, 106, 107, 109, 111, 116	10, 56, 58, 86, 88, 89, 118, 121, 124, 125, 126, 127, 128, 129, 130, 131, 133, 134, 135, 136, 137

Standards-Based SCIENCE Graphic Organizers, Rubrics, and Writing Prompts for Middle Grade Students

Suggestions for Using Graphic Organizers to Integrate Science into the Total Curriculum

1. Use concept webs or other advanced organizers to explain scientific ideas as they relate to historical events or current happenings.

   Example: Give a speech on pollution or endangered species.

2. Construct flowcharts or diagrams to show processes for completing a specific task related to gathering and disseminating facts and/or information about a scientific issue of concern to people of your age.

   Example: Use a flowchart to plan and develop a research project on conserving our natural resources for the next generation.

3. Design a puppet show storyboard that shows parts of an important event currently affecting global warming, world population, or some other scientific topic of social significance. Remember that a storyboard does not attempt to show all of the scenes in a story, but merely serves as an outline for the major people, places, and events.

4. Design an explanatory chart to show an audience the relationships, sequences, or positions that exist within an institution, group, or collection of data. Consider any topic for this chart, from the types of food chains in natural habitats, to the interactions of countries in sharing technological advances.

5. Use one or more graphic organizers to prepare a presentation. Some graphic organizers to consider are a Concept Builder, a Storyboard, a Venn diagram, a Fishbone, or a Flowchart. This type of presentation is designed to appeal to a person's ability to reason or to a person's ability to feel emotions. Arrange your arguments so that they:
   (1) ask a question and then answer it,
   (2) relate an anecdote, observation, or experience,
   (3) state a fact or statistic.

Standards-Based SCIENCE Graphic Organizers, Rubrics, and Writing Prompts for Middle Grade Students

6. Use a Book Report organizer to plan a report on a biography of a famous scientific person. As you prepare the report, think about your reactions to the events in the historical figure's life that please or bother you, situations that surprise or dazzle you, and obstacles that challenge or disappoint you.

7. Use Venn diagrams to compare and contrast people, places, and socially significant scientific happenings being studied.

   Example: Compare and contrast the development of Alexander Graham Bell's invention of the telephone with the development of the process of pasteurization discovered by Louis Pasteur.

8. Construct line graphs, picot graphs, bar graphs, or circle graphs to organize and present data related to scientific observations, research findings, or community poll results.

9. Use time lines to establish the chronology of important scientific events such as the sequence of events leading up to man landing on the moon, the history of the AIDS virus, or the development of the computer.

10. Identify cause-and-effect situations and construct a cause-and-effect chart to show the sequence and impact.

    Example: Graphically show the influence of technology in today's schools on the workplace of tomorrow.

Standards-Based SCIENCE Graphic Organizers, Rubrics, and Writing Prompts for Middle Grade Students

Criteria for Creating Your Own Rubric

Excellent

My portfolio, project, or task
1. is complete.
2. is well-organized.
3. is visually exciting.
4. shows much evidence of multiple resources.
5. shows much evidence of problem solving, decision making, and higher-order thinking skills.
6. reflects enthusiasm for the subject.
7. contains additional work beyond the requirements.
8. communicates effectively what I have learned in keeping with my learning objectives.
9. includes highly efficient assessment tools and makes ample provisions for meta cognitive reflection.
10. has identified many future learning goals in keeping with my own needs and interests.

Good

My portfolio, project, or task
1. is complete.
2. is well-organized.
3. is interesting.
4. shows some evidence of multiple resources.
5. shows some evidence of problem solving, decision making, and higher-order thinking skills.
6. reflects some interest for the topic.
7. contains a small amount of work beyond the requirements.
8. communicates some things I have learned in keeping with my learning objectives.
9. includes effective assessment tools and reflective comments.
10. has identified some future learning goals in keeping with my own needs and interests.

Needs Improvement

My portfolio, project, or task
1. is incomplete.
2. is poorly organized.
3. is not very interesting to others.
4. shows little or almost no evidence of multiple resources.
5. shows little or almost no evidence of problem solving, decision making, and higher-order thinking skills.
6. reflects little interest in the subject.
7. contains no additional work beyond the minimum requirements.
8. communicates few things that I have truly learned in keeping with my objectives.
9. includes few examples of self assessment tools and reflective comments.
10. has identified no future learning goals in keeping with my own needs and interests.

Standards-Based SCIENCE Graphic Organizers, Rubrics, and Writing Prompts for Middle Grade Students

Copyright ©2001 by Incentive Publications, Inc.
Nashville, TN.

Outline for Creating Your Own Rubric

Use this outline and the criteria for creating your own rubric to create a holistic or analytic rubric for evaluating a portfolio, project, or task. A holistic rubric assigns levels of performance with descriptors for each level. An analytic rubric assigns levels of performance with numerical points allocated for every descriptor at each level.

Excellent Levels

Descriptors: Points Awarded:

_____   _____

_____   _____

_____   _____

Good Levels

Descriptors: Points Awarded:

_____   _____

_____   _____

_____   _____

Needs Improvement

Descriptors: Points Awarded:

_____   _____

_____   _____

_____   _____

NOTE: You can add additional levels and descriptors as needed. You can also create your own labels for the levels and use such categories as: Exemplary Achievement, Commendable Achievement, Limited Evidence of Achievement, and Minimal Achievement or simply top levels, medium levels, or needs improvement levels.

Comments by Student: _____

_____

Signed _____ Date _____

Comments by Teacher: _____

_____

Signed _____ Date _____

Performance, Project, or Task
Independent Study Contract

Title: _____

Topic: _____

Beginning date of work_____

Planned completion/delivery date _____

Goals and/or learning objectives to be accomplished _____

_____

Statement of problems to be researched/studied _____

_____

Format _____

Information/data/resources needed _____

_____

Technical help needed_____

_____

Special equipment and/or materials needed _____

_____

Visual aids and/or artifacts planned _____

_____

Intended audience_____

Method of assessment _____

Student Signature _____ Date: _____

Teacher Signature _____ Date: _____

Standards-Based SCIENCE Graphic Organizers, Rubrics,
and Writing Prompts for Middle Grade Students

Student Self-Assessment Checklist for Participation in Science Investigations

	Poor		Fair		Excellent
1. Shows active participation in planned activities	1	2	3	4	5
2. Organizes equipment and materials for experimentation	1	2	3	4	5
3. Identifies variables before beginning experimentation	1	2	3	4	5
4. Follows a scientific method and applies scientific process skills	1	2	3	4	5
5. Formulates a hypothesis	1	2	3	4	5
6. Applies observation skills	1	2	3	4	5
7. Applies classification skills	1	2	3	4	5
8. Records data accurately	1	2	3	4	5
9. Demonstrates scientific curiosity	1	2	3	4	5
10. Understands use of scientific terms and symbols	1	2	3	4	5
11. Reads, interprets and constructs graphs and tables	1	2	3	4	5
12. Recognizes patterns and relationships	1	2	3	4	5
13. Predicts outcomes	1	2	3	4	5
14. Interprets test results by synthesizing information	1	2	3	4	5
15. Formulates reliable conclusions	1	2	3	4	5
16. Applies problem solving techniques	1	2	3	4	5
17. Demonstrates effective use of time	1	2	3	4	5
18. Shows care and ability with equipment	1	2	3	4	5
19. Follows safety precautions	1	2	3	4	5
20. Shows care and ability in lab cleanup	1	2	3	4	5

From Science Yellow Pages by The Kids' Stuff™ People, Incentive Publications, Inc.

Judging Criteria for A Science Fair Project

1. Scientific Investigations—40 points

   - Is the purpose/hypothesis stated on the display?

   - Is the procedure used in developing and obtaining the solution or results explained?

   - Is the method of data acquisition or analysis explained?

   - Does the data support the conclusion?

2. Creative Ability—15 points

   - Did the student design and construct any equipment?

   - Does this project display originality?

   - Is the data presented uniquely?

   - How creative is the display?

3. Thoroughness—20 points

   - How many times was the investigation performed?

   - Does the display physically demonstrate the operation or results?

   - Have the variables affecting the outcome been identified?

   - Are accurate amounts of materials listed?

4. Skill—15 points

   - Is the demonstrated skill commensurate with the student's age and grade level?

5. Clarity/Neatness—10 points

   - Is the written material clearly presented?
     Is the data easy to understand?

   - Is the display well-organized and attractive?

   - Is the material readable and arranged in a logical manner?

From Science Yellow Pages by The Kids' Stuff™ People, Incentive Publications, Inc.

Bloom's Taxonomy of Cognitive Thinking Skills for Students

Bloom's Taxonomy of Cognitive Development is a model that can help you learn how to think critically and systematically. (*Taxonomy* is another word for *structure* or *schemata*.) This taxonomy provides a way to organize thinking skills into six levels. The first level is the most basic, or simplest, level of thinking, and the last level is the most challenging, or most complex, level of thinking.

BLOOM'S TAXONOMY OF CRITICAL THINKING SKILLS

KNOWLEDGE LEVEL:
Students thinking at this level are asked to memorize, remember, and recall previously learned material. Some common verbs or behaviors for this level are: define, list, identify, label, name, recall, record, draw, recite, and reproduce.

COMPREHENSION LEVEL:
Students thinking at this level are asked to demonstrate their ability to understand the meaning of material learned and to express that meaning in their own words. Some common verbs or behaviors for this level are: explain, describe, summarize, give examples, classify, find, measure, prepare, re-tell, reword, rewrite, and show.

APPLICATION LEVEL:
Students thinking at this level are asked to use learned material in a situation different from the situation in which the material was taught. Some common verbs or behaviors for this level are: apply, compute, construct, develop, discuss, generalize, interview, investigate, model, perform, plan, present, produce, prove, solve, and use.

ANALYSIS LEVEL:
Students thinking at this level are asked to break down material (ideas and concepts) into its component parts so that the organization and relationships between parts is better recognized and understood. Some common verbs or behaviors for this level are: compare and contrast, criticize, debate, determine, diagram, differentiate, discover, draw conclusions, examine, infer, search, survey, and sort.

SYNTHESIS LEVEL:
Students thinking at this level are asked to put together parts of the material to form a new and different whole. Synthesis is the exact opposite of analysis. Some common verbs or behaviors for this level are: build, combine, create, design, imagine, invent, make-up, produce, propose, and present.

EVALUATION LEVEL:
Students thinking at this level are asked to judge the value of material (a statement, novel, poem, research finding, fact) for a given purpose. All judgments are to be based on a set of clearly defined criteria whose outcomes can be defended or validated. Some common verbs or behaviors for this level are: assess, critique, defend, evaluate, grade, judge, measure, rank, recommend, select, test, validate, and verify.

Standards-Based SCIENCE Graphic Organizers, Rubrics, and Writing Prompts for Middle Grade Students

Outline Arranged According to Bloom's Taxonomy for Developing a Project or Lesson Plan for a Science Topic

Topic: _____

KNOWLEDGE

1. List questions that you would like to answer about the topic.

2. Identify and define key words or terms related to the topic.

3. List resources that can be used to locate information related to the topic.

COMPREHENSION

1. Make a study plan for finding out all you can about the topic.

2. Summarize important facts and/or concepts you need to find.

3. Describe ways that you might share the information you gather.

APPLICATION

1. Plan an interview with someone very knowledgeable about the topic.

2. Design a model to show something important about the topic.

3. Plan to make an experiment to demonstrate a key idea related to the topic.

ANALYSIS

1. Compare and contrast some aspect of the topic with that of a related topic.

2. Separate the topic into several subtopics.

3. Plan a survey to demonstrate what your classmates know about the topic.

SYNTHESIS

1. Create a list of predictions related to the topic.

2. Compose a poem or short story about the topic.

3. Design a series of drawings or diagrams to demonstrate facts and or concepts related to the topic.

EVALUATION

1. Determine the most important facts and/or concepts you have learned about the topic. Order the facts or concepts from most important to least important, giving reasons for your choices.

2. Criticize a resource you used and give recommendations for improving it.

Standards-Based SCIENCE Graphic Organizers, Rubrics, and Writing Prompts for Middle Grade Students

Copyright ©2001 by Incentive Publications, Inc. Nashville, TN.

Periodic Table Talk

KNOWLEDGE:
List the elements of the periodic table.

COMPREHENSION:
Explain how the periodic table can be of great use to scientists, environmentalists, or archeologists.

APPLICATION:
Demonstrate how you might use the periodic table in a science project, a science fair, or a science lab.

ANALYSIS:
Compare and contrast any two elements of the periodic table. Do this in graph or chart form.

SYNTHESIS:
Devise a simple lesson plan to teach a friend something about the periodic table. Your lesson plan should have the following parts:
- Objective
- Time
- Materials Needed
- Procedure
- Follow-up

Use it to educate your friend.

EVALUATION:
Judge the quality of your lesson plan by answering the following questions.

1. Were my objectives relevant and realistic in terms of intent and number?

2. Was I enthusiastic in my delivery?

3. Was I well prepared and well organized?

4. Were my directions clear and to the point?

5. Would I do anything differently next time when presenting this lesson?

*From **Tools, Treasures, & Measures for Middle Grade Success** by Imogene Forte and Sandra Schurr, Incentive Publications, Inc.*

Standards-Based SCIENCE Graphic Organizers, Rubrics, and Writing Prompts for Middle Grade Students

Outline For Developing A Unit On Any Science Topic

Developing a science unit on a topic of your choice is easier than you think. Just choose your topic and then select one or more tasks from each level of Bloom's Taxonomy (below) to create a teaching and learning unit.

TOPIC _____

KNOWLEDGE

1. List five to ten questions that you would like to answer about the topic.
2. Identify five to ten key words or terms related to the topic and write their definitions.
3. Name three to five specific sources for information about the topic.

COMPREHENSION

1. Outline a plan for finding out all you can about the topic.
2. Summarize what you would like to know most about the topic.
3. Describe five to ten ways that you might share acquired information.

APPLICATION

1. Interview someone with knowledge of the topic.
2. Make a model to show something important about the topic.
3. Conduct an experiment to demonstrate a key idea related to the topic.

ANALYSIS

1. Compare and contrast some aspect of your topic with that of another topic.
2. Divide your topic into several sub-topics.
3. Conduct a survey to show how others feel about the topic.

SYNTHESIS

1. Create a list of predictions related to the topic.
2. Compose a poem or story about the topic.
3. Design a series of drawings or diagrams to show facts about the topic.

EVALUATION

1. Determine the five most important facts you have learned about the topic. Rank order them from most important to least important, giving reasons for your first choice.
2. Criticize a resource you used to find out more information about the topic and give at least three recommendations for improving it.

Standards-Based SCIENCE Graphic Organizers, Rubrics, and Writing Prompts for Middle Grade Students

Book Report
Outline For Use with
Any Science Project

DIRECTIONS: Select a non-fiction book on the science topic of your choice and use it to complete the activities below.

KNOWLEDGE

  1. Record the answers to each of these questions:

      What is the title of the book?

      Who wrote the book?

      When was the book published?

      Where did you locate the book?

COMPREHENSION

  2. Summarize the main ideas or facts found in the book.

APPLICATION

  3. Select several key words or terms from the book and classify them in some way.

ANALYSIS

  4. Compare your book with another book on the same topic. How are the books alike and how are they different?

SYNTHESIS

  5. Suppose that you were to write a new book on this topic. Create an original book jacket for your masterpiece.

EVALUATION

  6. Would you recommend the book to anyone else?
     Give three to five reasons for your choice.

_____

_____

_____

_____

_____

Standards-Based SCIENCE Graphic Organizers, Rubrics, and Writing Prompts for Middle Grade Students

Experiment Form
for Use with Any Science Topic

KNOWLEDGE

List the materials used in this experiment.
Materials:

_____

_____

_____

_____

COMPREHENSION

Outline the procedure for conducting this experiment.
Procedure:

1. _____

2. _____

3. _____

4. _____

5. _____

6. _____

APPLICATION

Record data observed and collected during your experiment in chart or graph form.
Data:

What I Did	What I Observed

Standards-Based SCIENCE Graphic Organizers, Rubrics, and Writing Prompts for Middle Grade Students

ANALYSIS

Examine your data and draw conclusions.
Conclusions:

1. _____

_____

2. _____

_____

3. _____

_____

SYNTHESIS

Create a series of "what if" statements about your data to show things that might be different should variables be changed.

What if . . . _____

_____

What if . . . _____

_____

What if . . . _____

_____

EVALUATION

Describe how you would rate the success of your experiment. Establish a set of criteria for measuring the results.

Findings	Measure of Success

Standards-Based SCIENCE Graphic Organizers, Rubrics, and Writing Prompts for Middle Grade Students

Teacher's
Science Curriculum Assessment

1. **My curriculum plan for the year is well organized to adhere to national and state standards, and to cover all the skills and content mandated for my grade level.**

   _____   _____   _____   _____
   Absolutely   I think so   I hope so   I don't know

   Notes/Comments: _____

   _____

2. **My curriculum plan allows room for meeting individual student needs.**

   _____   _____   _____   _____
   Absolutely   I think so   I hope so   I don't know

   Notes/Comments: _____

   _____

3. **My plan includes a good balance of directed instruction, large and small group work including cooperative learning and flexible groups, and independent study.**

   _____   _____   _____   _____
   Absolutely   I think so   I hope so   I don't know

   Notes/Comments: _____

   _____

4. **Opportunities for student participation and the employment of active learning strategies are prevalent throughout my plan.**

   _____   _____   _____   _____
   Absolutely   I think so   I hope so   I don't know

   Notes/Comments: _____

   _____

5. I have planned for authentic assessment of student progress as well as for any required traditional methods of assessment such as standardized tests and letter grades where required by the school system.

| _____ | _____ | _____ | _____ |
| Absolutely | I think so | I hope so | I don't know |

Notes/Comments: _____

_____

_____

6. My plan is feasible in terms of time and resources available.

| _____ | _____ | _____ | _____ |
| Absolutely | I think so | I hope so | I don't know |

Notes/Comments: _____

_____

_____

7. I have planned blocks of time to allow flexibility for maximizing those "teachable moments" that encourage spontaneously and foster creativity.

| _____ | _____ | _____ | _____ |
| Absolutely | I think so | I hope so | I don't know |

Notes/Comments: _____

_____

_____

8. My curriculum goals are realistic and achievable yet ambitious in terms of student achievement.

| _____ | _____ | _____ | _____ |
| Absolutely | I think so | I hope so | I don't know |

Notes/Comments: _____

_____

_____

Standards-Based SCIENCE Graphic Organizers, Rubrics, and Writing Prompts for Middle Grade Students

9. My plan provides enrichment activities and time for reflection appropriate to the age level and subject I teach.

| Absolutely | I think so | I hope so | I don't know |

Notes/Comments: _____

_____

10. My plan includes provision for parent communication.

| Absolutely | I think so | I hope so | I don't know |

Notes/Comments: _____

_____

11. My plan is consistent with school goals, administrative expectancies, and will allow for cooperation and partnership with the larger school community.

| Absolutely | I think so | I hope so | I don't know |

Notes/Comments: _____

_____

12. I have reviewed my plan carefully and feel that it is a truly excellent program.

| Absolutely | I think so | I hope so | I don't know |

Notes/Comments: _____

_____

Reflection:

After considering the soundness of my curriculum plan for the year as reflected by this assessment tool, I feel that I should make the following additions, deletions, or modifications.

_____

_____

_____

Date: _____

Standards-Based SCIENCE Graphic Organizers, Rubrics, and Writing Prompts for Middle Grade Students

Copyright ©2001 by Incentive Publications, Inc.
Nashville, TN.

Bibliography

The All-New Science Mind Stretchers. Imogene Forte and Sandra Schurr. Nashville, Incentive Publications Inc., 1996

A to Z Community and Service Learning. Imogene Forte and Sandra Schurr. Nashville, Incentive Publications Inc., 1997

BASIC/Not Boring Earth & Space Science Grades 6-8+. Imogene Forte and Marge Frank. Nashville, Incentive Publications Inc., 1997

BASIC/Not Boring Life Science Grades 6-8+. Imogene Forte and Marge Frank. Nashville, Incentive Publications Inc., 1997

BASIC/Not Boring Physical Science Grades 6-8+. Imogene Forte and Marge Frank. Nashville, Incentive Publications Inc., 1997

The Definitive Middle School Guide. Imogene Forte and Sandra Schurr. Nashville, Incentive Publications Inc., 1993

Ecology Green Pages. The Kids' Stuff™ People. Nashville, Incentive Publications Inc., 1993

Graphic Organizers and Planning Outlines. Imogene Forte and Sandra Schurr. Nashville, Incentive Publications Inc., 1996

The Green Team. Dorothy Michener. Nashville, Incentive Publications Inc., 1993

How to Write a Great Research Paper. Leland Graham and Darriel Ledbetter. Nashville, Incentive Publications Inc., 1994

Integrating Instruction in Science. Imogene Forte and Sandra Schurr. Nashville, Incentive Publications Inc., 1996

Interdisciplinary Units and Projects for Thematic Instruction. Imogene Forte and Sandra Schurr. Nashville, Incentive Publications Inc., 1994

Reports Students Love to Write and Teachers Love to Read. Imogene Forte and Sandra Schurr. Nashville, Incentive Publications Inc., 1999

Use That Computer! Lucinda Johnston, Howard Johnston, and James Forde. Nashville, Incentive Publications Inc., 2001

Science Yellow Pages. The Kids' Stuff™ People. Nashville, Incentive Publications Inc., 1993

Wow, What a Team! Randy Thompson and Dorothy VanderJagt. Nashville, Incentive Publications Inc., 2001

Index

Standards-Based SCIENCE Graphic Organizers, Rubrics, and Writing Prompts for Middle Grade Students

Copyright ©2001 by Incentive Publications, Inc. Nashville, TN.